M000278683

SUDDEN VIOLENCE
THE ART OF SAN SOO

MASTER GREG JONES

PALADIN PRESS
BOULDER, COLORADO

Sudden Violence: The Art of San Soo
by Master Greg Jones

Copyright © 1988 by Greg Jones

ISBN 0-87364-465-4
Printed in the United States of America

Published by Paladin Press, a division of
Paladin Enterprises, Inc., P.O. Box 1307,
Boulder, Colorado 80306, USA.
(303) 443-7250

Direct inquiries and/or orders to the above address.

Illustrations by Lea S. Nash

Photographs by Casey Dale and Randy Kaizer

CONTENTS

DEDICATION

   This book is dedicated to my brother Mike, now deceased. He and I began training in the martial arts at the same time and continued on through our black belts.
   Without a doubt, this book would not have been possible for me to write were it not for the pragmatic approach and aggressive training my brother inspired in me . . . and that I now share with you.

ACKNOWLEDGMENTS

When a project such as this book comes to a close and you're expected to thank those that were the most helpful to you, you're left with a pervasive feeling that you've left someone out. If this proves to be the case—and you certainly know who you are—please forgive me. I'll always be grateful for the role you've played in the writing of this book, and ultimately in my life, even if I've overlooked you here. Thank you.

I'd first like to acknowledge my instructors and role models in my martial development, including my first instructor through a black belt level, Jerry Druckerman, and his instructor, Bill Lassiter, who inspired in me the direction and awe I needed as the training became more aggressive and demanding; Al Rubin, who taught me through my degrees through Master, and yet, so very much more. Al Rubin died in April 1987 of leukemia. I'll always be indebted to Master Rubin for his role in my martial skills, but more importantly to me, he taught me the value of humor, honor, pride...and friendship (thanks Al). And of course, Jimmy H. Woo for sharing his art and his life with us. Kung fu san soo *is* Jimmy H. Woo.

As for the actual production of this book, I'd like to thank those who participated in this venture; including my wife Cheryl and my sons Greg and Chris for their support and modeling; Casey Dale for his exhaustive work as photographer/model; Randy Kaizer for his photographs and cooperation; Lea S. Nash for her terrific drawings; friends and models Bruce Fountain and children Alyssa and Jordy; Adam Wyatt; Kathy Kallen; Terry Abeyta; Dana Gardner; Matt Freer; the family of Darkroom Specialties of Eugene, Oregon for the film development; and finally, the folks at Paladin Press: Rebecca Herr, Editorial Director, for her guidance and patience with me; Jon Ford for his help and tactful input; and the rest of the staff at Paladin who put this project together.

PREFACE

To what extremes are you willing to go to ensure your own safety? Can you actually put out someone's eyes, crush a throat, break a neck, fracture a kneecap or spine, smash a groin, or do anything else that will bring about sudden and excruciating pain? Do you believe you have it within you to be able to take a man's life with little or no hesitation if a situation warrants it? These are not rhetorical questions; it's crucial to your personal safety to assess and answer them as honestly as you possibly can.

Whether you can or cannot go to these extremes has no bearing on whether you view yourself as a good or bad person, only that if you can't bring yourself to injure someone who threatens your life, you'll be as victimized by your ethics as by your attacker!

You can apply the principles contained in this book to stop an attacker from his initial or secondary attack, but unless you're willing to hurt him, you may as well not defend yourself in the first place; your death or injuries will be inevitable.

In the final analysis, you're only as safe as you allow yourself to be. If you feel you may be safe after having purchased a firearm, you will be insofar as you're willing to pull the trigger. Admittedly this is something you cannot know, up to and until you will actually have to shoot someone; but you should know that there are simply too many people who are shot with their own weapon because they waited too long to act in their own defense, naively hoping the threat would simply go away. As with a gun, self-defense training is only useful if it is used!

When I decided to begin training in the martial arts for self-defense, I searched for an art that would best serve my personal needs. This was not an easy search. Though my needs were simple, the many and varied styles were complex and confusing. I had no want or need for trophies or cheering crowds, no need for hands of stone, no need to look pretty while wreaking mayhem on my attacker, and I certainly had no need for bowing or rituals. All I ever wanted from any particular style was for it to work. I wanted the confidence in myself and techniques so that I might face any situation calmly, without being plagued by self-doubt, uncertainty, rapid pulse, or shaky knees (sound familiar?).

The training methods of the san soo style of kung fu met and far exceeded my requirements and expectations. Moreover, this method of self-defense gave me the ability and confidence to protect myself and family in practically any given situation, not by using brawn, speed, cat-like agility, animal instincts, or mystical powers, but by applying logical principles and spontaneously following through with simple and direct techniques.

San soo was brought to the United States in 1959 by Grandmaster Jimmy H. Woo, but the art's origins are many centuries old. It was developed in China at the Quan Yem monastery in Hoy Song, Canton. Chin'Moon Dan, the great, great, great grandfather of Master Woo, left the monastery as a priest. With him, in addition to the teachings and experience he had gained as a priest, were two valuable books that came into his possession about the fighting techniques of san soo.

Realizing what a powerful source he possessed, he decided to keep the art a secret. He taught only the members of his family after having sworn them to secrecy. The art was then passed down from generation to generation, from father to son, uncle to nephew, cousin to cousin.

Grandmaster Woo began his formal training at the age of seven and has continued to teach his beloved art for well over fifty years. He is a proud man who instills pride in others, and yet remains devoid of the arrogance normally associated with a proud person.

The colorful background and rich history of Grandmaster Woo and the art of san soo is a fascinating story. However, out of deference, it is a story that is best left for him to tell. I will instead confine my text to the application of the principles and techniques of this highly efficient fighting art.

Quite simply, students of san soo are taught to respect the other man as an equal, regardless of rank, and therefore not underestimate his abilities. Rather than presume ourselves to be superior fighters because of our experience and training, we will presume the other man to be the superior fighter, *but not give him a chance to prove it!* This is the premise for the title of this book and the basic concept of realistic self-defense training.

The art of kung fu san soo (which the International Kung Fu San Soo Association defines as "the articulate use of the body for self-defense") is comprised of five "families" of diverse, yet interrelated facets. These families are:

1. ***Tsoi Ga.*** This family of san soo concerns the art of striking (Tsoi is translated as "punching and kicking"). In addition to the many ways of striking with the hands, I think a great many martial artists would be surprised at the variety of kicks employed in san soo. The number and types of kicks a san soo martial artist uses would be enough to fill a book all by itself. But Tsoi Ga is also about striking in combinations of punches, kicks, elbow and knee strikes, as well as incorporating other body areas as striking surfaces so that the well-rounded student doesn't become dependent upon just punching or kicking.

2. ***Li Ga.*** Li is translated as "leverage," and this facet of

san soo training delves into leverage, throws, leverage-type throws, and takedowns incorporating leverages. This particular aspect comes into its own when dealing in close with someone, as in a grappling situation, or to control an opponent by putting a lock on his joints and limbs.

3. *Hoi Ga.* Hoi Ga is the study and application of pressure points, pass and crippling points, and the ways and means of striking vital areas to bring about pain, injury, or death (Hoi is translated as "pressure points"). This is a fascinating area to study because it effectively demonstrates that when dealing with a large opponent, you can attack specific areas accurately and with force rather than having to cope with his greater size and strength.

4. *Fut Ga.* The fourth family of san soo—translated as "psychology" or "internal power"—covers the psychology of men and fighting, proper fighting attitudes, and strong offensive techniques. Yet Fut Ga goes deeper than this, also drawing upon internal power, proper breathing, balance in movement, and sudden execution of decided action to end a fight almost before it's begun. When Fut Ga is fully grasped and applied, it instills in the student a very certain and profound "predator" attitude. This sensitivity compels the student to deal with the opponent at the first hint of an attack.

5. *Hung Ga.* This area deals with the physical conditioning of the body in order for it to perform up to its maximum potential. The physical dynamics of Hung Ga include dynamic tension exercises, forms, technique workouts, and the usage of kinetic energy for external power. Hung is translated as "physical dynamics" or "external power."

Because training in the art of san soo largely consists of the application of principle, you learn to *intelligently* apply yourself to any situation, which is more valuable than committing hundreds of lessons to memory. It isn't necessary to be a skilled fighter who relies on speed, strength, and conditioned responses when you can be more effective utilizing *knowledge.* Thus, consider the study of this or any other martial art the same as studying physics; your knowledge is your strength, more so than physical prowess.

To better illustrate my point, imagine that you could return to prehistoric times. This done, envision a group of cavemen embroiled in a contest of strength. Each in turn attempts to move a huge boulder and is failing miserably; one caveman tries to shove it, another tries to lift it, and another puts his back to it and tries to shove with his legs. Your turn; you roll a smaller boulder up to the larger one and utilize a heavy limb to facilitate a lever and fulcrum. The boulder is moved and the cavemen cheer your awesome strength.

They fail to see that you had simply applied a basic principle of physics, and thus you applied knowledge. When this analogy is used in a martial context, we hear of black belts and professional boxers and wrestlers who are touted as being real tough guys. Are they? Maybe so, but it's their knowledge of fighting skills that makes them tough, not necessarily their physical attributes.

Kung fu san soo incorporates the principles of line, distance, angle, and movement of attack. It's based on a combination of techniques that can be changed instantly to suit the situation and that do not follow a set pattern. The combinations consist of punching, kicking, using knees and elbows, biting and gouging, hair-pulling control techniques, leverage movements and takedowns, and much more. These strikes and blows are directed to the weak and vulnerable spots of the body, points that are classified as nerve centers and pass (death and permanent crippling) points.

As previously mentioned, the concept of accurately striking the vulnerable points of the body is based on the fact that you want to avoid fighting the great bulk of a large opponent, but rather attack specific places that will neutralize his mass and girth. Picture being confronted by a large, powerfully built man. Understandably most people would be intimidated; *but anatomically he is no different than you.* There are no muscles to protect his eyes, throat, bridge of the nose, groin, shin, knees, or spinal column; he is literally as vulnerable as you are.

To supplement your study of martial arts and self-defense, you should seriously consider the study of anatomy. Become familiar with the skeletal, neural, vascular, and muscle systems; their placement and their functions. This will not only give you a familiarity with potential targets, but should at the same time acquaint you with the truly amazing works of fine machinery that our bodies are, and thus the sanctity of life.

In order to best utilize this book, you will need the assistance of a partner who will be as willing to invest as much time and concentration to the study as you are. You and your partner should schedule your training periods to coincide on a frequent basis. Arrange to devote your total concentration to the study of this text; I would expect it from you if you were in my class, and I expect no less because you're reading my book.

At times, your training may become painful when you apply various techniques. You can learn from pain in the sense that you can understand exactly what you're inflicting on your opponent by having the same technique applied to you. You will have felt what he is feeling so that if you are ever involved in a self-defense situation, you can alter the degree of pain from uncomfortable to excruciating with the blink of an eye.

Much can be learned from san soo, no matter what style you're currently involved in (if you're already training). The only thing I ask of you, is to keep an open mind while reading this material. At the risk of leaning toward cliché, think of that oft-quoted Zen saying: "Before you can taste my tea, you must first empty your cup."
cup."

Chapter 1

PRINCIPLES AND APPLICATIONS OF KUNG FU SAN SOO

When exploring a particular style of the martial arts, many people actually ask themselves, "What's in it for me?" They also want to know what makes it unique from other martial art styles.

Because the san soo style of kung fu closely approximates street fighting conditions rather than sport fighting, it's only logical that we would have different principles to apply than a martial art that emphasizes the latter.

Styles that encompass a broad and very often conflicting scope would necessarily have a wide latitude in principles and their application. For instance, a style that can be considered both traditional while encouraging competitiveness for tournaments would by necessity entail many principles and concepts in order to maintain a balance.

Essentially, san soo can be broken down into four common denominators or, more aptly, conditions that are universally present regardless of technique or artist. These are the principles of line, distance, angle, and movement. There are additional principles to support these four, but they're more peripheral than fundamental (yet they still play an integral role in the application of the techniques).

San soo principles are such that a small, light person has as much opportunity to utilize the body to achieve maximum power as a larger athlete. The physics involved are time-tested, sound, and appropriate for the circumstances. Because of this, practitioners of the art are better equipped to defend themselves against opponents with more fighting experience or who are bigger and stronger.

In sport fighting, the opponents are of similar size and weight. In a self-defense situation, the opponent may tower over you and be much heavier; this is the opponent you need to learn about and train for. An opponent in a street situation will almost always view himself as bigger and tougher than you or he wouldn't consider attacking in the first place.

When you see a large, powerfully built man, you may feel intimidated even though you have no direct threat posed to you. Some people even feel physically weakened when merely in the presence of a huge man. If you feel this way, you inflict upon yourself a handicap of being helpless and ineffective in the face of what potentially could be a serious and violent encounter. If an aggressor senses that you're already frightened of him, it will only reinforce his decision to attack.

This is the predator in man; it is a very real and primal instinct that we use to assess who does or does not pose a threat to us. This evaluation takes place in the first instant that one man meets another and determines what course of action he will or won't take, depending upon whether the other man displays anger, fear, or indifference. If you display fear signals—either in word, action, or deed—an aggressive or angry person might feel compelled to attack where he otherwise wouldn't. It's important that you remember this.

While it's true that a large man can be dangerous in that he can probably deliver a powerful blow, it's entirely possible for a smaller person to be able to deliver an even stronger punch if he utilizes his body weight when delivering the strike.

When a person punches, he'll usually step forward and punch *after* the foot has come to rest. In doing so, the person will actually be punching with only a portion of the power he could be hitting with if he used his body weight. This is because when the feet are planted, you're only hitting with the weight and speed of your arm (aside from upper body torque). However, if you punch *as* your foot sets to the floor, you'll be hitting with the weight of your body as well.

You can prove this to yourself on a heavy punching bag. Stand stationary and punch, keeping your knuckles in line with your forearm. Then step and punch, hitting the bag as your foot sets down. Punch the bag again, this time, pivoting your torso sideways to the bag as you hit; this will enable you to add torque from the waist and torso to increase the power in your punch.

Several traditional styles of karate instruct students to keep their shoulders square and to face the opponent as they strike. *Don't do this!* This will rob you of the power you could otherwise achieve. Tradition is fine for many people in many ways, but when it limits your potential, it's time to move on.

To better understand the folly of punching with your shoulders square to an opponent, you'll need your partner.

Have your partner face you with his or her shoulders square to your own. Extend your right arm and fist to your partner's nose as though you were punching, and have your partner do the same to you at the same time; be sure each of you have the fist pressed to the other's nose. Now turn your torso sideways to your partner (Fig. 1).

See the added reach you have over him? Not only that, you'll have considerably more power. This principle applies to kicks as well. If your hips are facing his, then you're just as vulnerable as he is. By pivoting your hips, you'll not only have superior reach, but more power in your kicks as well (Fig. 2). So as you can see, you don't necessarily have to be strong to have power; simply utilize your own natural reach and weight when striking.

Another test you can use to prove the validity of stepping in to your punch is a progressive series of pushes. Have your partner stand in front of you at arm's reach. Stand flat footed and push him as hard as you can. Didn't move very far, did

Figure 1

Figure 2

Figure 3

he? Now with your arm extended, pick up your knee and lean into him. Better isn't it? On the third try, after having lifted your knee, set your foot down as you shove him (Fig. 3).

If you take these same lessons and apply them to a punch, you'll be well on your way to putting your body weight into each and every blow. That's the ideal to work toward; employing your body *as a unit* to ward off or deliver strikes quickly.

Speed is important in any martial art style, but it isn't absolutely essential. As you don't have to be strong to be powerful, you also don't have to be extremely fast to be effective; this brings us to the distance principle.

If you were to stand toe-to-toe with a potential attacker, you are almost certain to be hit should he decide to strike you. The reason for this is a lack of sufficient reaction time. By the time your eye detects a movement and the brain decides a course of action, it will be too late. However, if you're at arm's distance from an opponent, your reaction time will increase greatly.

To prove this to yourself, have your partner stand toe-to-toe with you. Instruct him to swat your hand away before you slap his shoulder (Fig. 4).

You should be able to hit his shoulder easily. This time stand at arm's length and try it again (Fig. 5).

This should prove to be more difficult for you. Now reverse roles and try to swat his slap away from a toe-to-toe position and then again at arm's distance.

Practice this exercise so that you are able to ascertain at a glance exactly where your "safe distance" is. When you're within easy reach of your opponent—ideally with your arm outstretched and your palm flat against his chest—you'll be able to close and smother his attack before it's fully launched. From this distance, you'll also be able to thwart any kick your opponent can throw simply by lifting your knee. If you allow him to gain more distance away from you, you'll have to deal with the full brunt of the kick rather than the initial movement (Fig. 6).

So, don't allow an opponent to get closer than your safe

Figure 4

Figure 5

Figure 6

distance (too little reaction time), and don't allow him to get too far outside your safe distance (too much room for him to kick).

You can apply the distance principle in a practical way; if you're in a crowded bar or at a party, simply imagine a circle around you an arm's length in distance, and be aware of who is on the edge of the circle or within it (Fig. 7). In this way, you can significantly reduce your chances of being "sucker punched." If someone you mistrust is too close to you, shift your position so that you can at least see him with your peripheral vision.

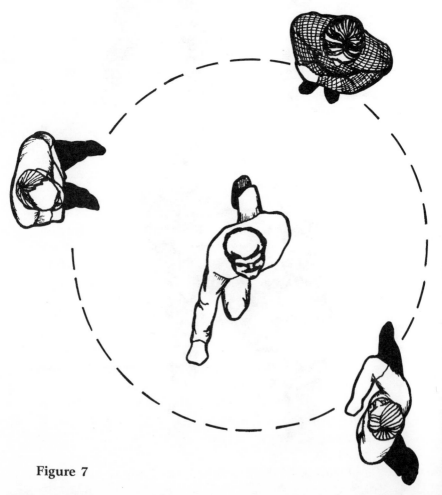

Figure 7

As you can see, controlling the distance between yourself and an opponent can play a vital role in determining the success or failure of a violent encounter. So remember, in any situation, immediately establish your safe distance (I know, one hundred miles away is safest, but we do have to be realistic). Conversely, if you intend to initiate the attack, *you* should invade *his* safe distance, thereby reducing his reaction time to your attack.

In self-defense, elaborate strategies, fancy footwork, and strenuous conditioning are not necessities. When you have to defend yourself spontaneously from a sudden violent attack, you won't be stretched, warmed up, psyched up, pumped up, or even ready. It will be an all-out ugly encounter with no one to watch, cheer you on, or to save you. It will in all probability be your worst nightmare come true. It's in this context, therefore, that I want to plant a seed in the back of your mind to adjust your concept of self-defense to self-attack.

San soo is an aggressive method of sudden violence in defense of one's self, and it works best when applied to certain lines of attack. These lines of attack are directed *into* an opponent instead of away. When you back away from an attack and simply block a punch, you really haven't accomplished very much; you haven't upset his balance, taken control of the encounter, or hurt him. All you succeed in doing when backing away is to prolong the situation.

In the art of kung fu san soo, you'll either remain stationary or step into (or into and alongside) an attacker (Fig. 8).

The importance of stepping in to punch an opponent instead of punching to keep an opponent at bay is best illustrated by thinking in terms of functional centers of gravity and circles of influence.

Look at the illustration in Figure 9 and you'll note that from above looking down, the man is both balanced and mobile because he occupies his own center of gravity. The reach he has with his arms and legs are his circles of influence—the area around himself within which he can effectively hit.

When two people come together and begin to fight, their

Figure 8

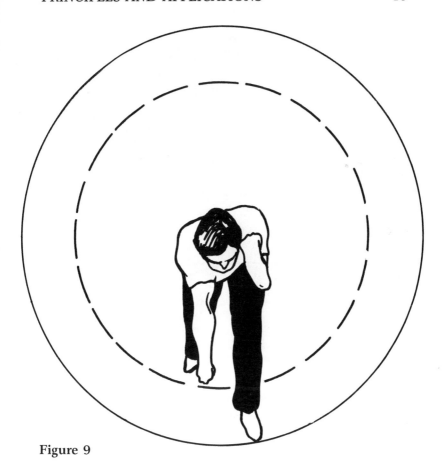

Figure 9

circles of influence will encompass that of the other and become enjoined in mutual punishment until one man either takes and occupies the other man's center of gravity or succumbs to the blows (Fig. 10).

By your closing the gap and invading his safe distance by stepping deeply enough into him to occupy his center of gravity, he will have no circles of influence because he has no way to direct his strikes. *You* will own his center of gravity and yours will be the only circles of influence (Fig. 11).

In order to fully grasp the significance of these principles, you must *do them!* The following drills will help familiarize you with the lines-of-attack principles that a san soo student must know instinctively to be most effective. Begin with your partner facing you at arm's length (safe distance), then lay a strip of masking tape from the middle of your feet to his. Now lay a strip directly alongside of him on both sides (see Fig. 8). Practice launching into your opponent along these lines. Keep yourself on top of or inside the lines to smother your opponent's movement when he tries to counter you.

Have your partner throw some slow punches as you get used to moving in on him. Initially it'll be easier for you to move into him if you remember to step to the left of him

Figure 10

Figure 11

with your left foot, and step to the right of him with your
right foot. You can step into the middle of him with either
foot and effectively jam his legs and bind his arms.

Depending upon the direction in which you step, you'll
have a different set of vulnerable points to strike. For
example, if your partner delivers a right punch and you step
to the left of him, you should be well past his punching arm
and leading leg; this will expose his right side as well as his
back and part of his frontal areas.

If your partner delivers another right punch and you step
to the right of him, his frontal areas will be exposed to you.
If he punches and you step directly into him after guiding
his punch past, you'll again have his frontal areas exposed
to you (Fig. 12).

Figure 12

As you step past him in either direction, be sure to use the correct hand to guide the punch safely past. If you step to the left of him, step with the left foot as you guide the punch with your left hand. Conversely, if you step to the right of him, step with the right foot and guide with the right hand.

In the beginning, it'll be less confusing for you if your partner punches with an extended punch; that is, he should step with the same side as he punches with (right punch, step with the right leg). This is a quick punch and it makes dealing with a looping "haymaker" blow a lot easier. After you feel comfortable dealing with an extended punch, you can vary the attacks.

If you feel uneasy about stepping into someone who's punching at you, you aren't alone. However, once you establish your distance, if you watch for telegraphic movement and deal with the action at once (preferably before the punch is fully launched), then stepping into an opponent won't be such a scary proposition.

If you're seriously studying san soo, it's imperative that you have a spontaneous working knowledge of the above line-of-attack principles and the corresponding movement skills so you'll be able to step deep enough and quickly enough to do the most damage and end a violent situation.

Presuming you've practiced line-of-attack entries, I'll point out several things that will make an already vital element of fighting even more cohesive (these are the peripheral principles mentioned earlier).

If you step into and alongside your opponent and can look him in the face, you'll be in a good position to attack—but so will he (Fig. 13a). If you hit a vital area immediately and press your attack, chances are good you won't be hit. If you don't score a decisive blow at the start, however, you'll be exposed and vulnerable to your opponent's counterattack.

Remember that if you step deep enough so that you're looking at the back or side of his head, you'll be well past anything he can readily throw at you (Fig. 13b). If you wait too long to attack him once you've stepped past, he can strike back at you with his elbow or leg. Additionally, you'll need

Figure 13a

Figure 13b

to bring up your trailing leg when you move in on your opponent; if you leave it too far back, you'll be vulnerable to a kick or sweep (Fig. 14a). By stepping deep enough and bringing up the trailing leg, you'll get sufficiently past him so that you can press your attack in relative safety (Fig. 14b).

As a final note (for the moment) on line of attack: If you can see that you're going to have to defend yourself and feel you must have a predetermined plan of action in order to be at ease about closing the gap, then pick a side to step in on and go for it. It's as simple as that.

If you choose to go to the right of your opponent, shift your weight to the left foot so you can push off to the right. If you decide to go to the left of him, shift your weight to your right foot. If the weight on your feet were evenly distributed, you'd have to shift-step-hit. It telegraphs your intention and takes time you won't have. Rather, shift your weight to the opposite foot you'll be stepping in on so that all you'll have to do is step-hit.

Don't be confused if the opponent throws punches opposite the foot he steps in with. Whether he delivers you a right or left punch (or kick), step in just the same.

In addition to stepping into an opponent, you should begin your movement from a relaxed posture, not a stance. Consider for a moment how much emphasis is placed on proper stances in the various martial art styles. While it's true that you can fight from a stance, you can fight better without one, if for no other reason than your arms and legs won't be committed to a specific position.

Let's examine a basic stance typical (with minor variations) to several styles of karate. The karate back stance involves stepping back with one leg, with the hand at the hip made into a fist. The other arm is extended down and above the front leg, with the hand made into a fist as well (Fig. 15).

Consider what you've done to yourself:

A) You've conveyed to your opponent that you're a martial artist of some kind, thereby making the task of defending yourself much more difficult because now he'll take you more seriously (no one will flee in terror after you assume a stance).

Figure 14a

Figure 14b

Figure 15

B) You've committed your arms and legs to a set position so that it will be difficult to move without telegraphing your intent.

C) Your mobility is now extremely limited.

D) It looks ridiculous and you'll feel like a fool when you're beaten!

Look at a simple kick delivered from this stance. Your weight is equally distributed so that in order to execute a front snap kick with your leading leg, you would either have to bring your front leg back to your rear leg to kick, or bring your rear leg to the front leg to kick (Fig. 16).

Either way you choose to do it, you'll telegraph your intent. However, if you're standing in a natural, relaxed manner with your legs no more than a shoulder's distance apart, you should be able to kick in any direction with minimal telegraphic movement (Fig. 17).

To take this a step further, try to dodge a blow from a classical stance. All you can do is duck your head and lean in another direction. If you stand in a natural posture, not only can you duck and dodge the blow, but you can step wide in any direction as well. When combined with the other principles, this becomes an extremely effective tactic to employ.

Another effective item you can add to your growing repertoire of san soo concepts is the incorporation of the pain principle. You can employ the use of pain to gain and keep control of your opponent. The ideal technique will bring about the highest degree of pain in the shortest amount of time, and with the least amount of effort.

When I speak of pain, I'm actually referring to the bodily reaction to pain. Unless you're a Yogi or some other type of physical phenomenon, you'll not be impassive when subjected to pain. We see that sudden and extreme pain causes an involuntary neuromuscular reaction—specifically the head and the hands follow the pain. For example, if you sit on a tack, your immediate response would be to leap out of the chair, bringing your hands to your butt and tilting back your head. Then you'd react rationally and see what it was you sat on and who put it there. If you stub your toe,

Figure 16

Figure 17

you're most likely going to hop around on one foot as you clutch at your toe with both hands, with your head bent toward your foot. If you cut or smash your finger, you'll automatically grab it with your other hand as you bend your head toward it (and give a new dimension to cussing). When struck in the back, the hands rush to the pain with the head tilted backward (Fig. 18).

As you can see, the head and the hands certainly do follow the pain, and therefore it will be to your decided advantage when defending yourself to make your opponent's body react accordingly (not unlike manipulating a marionette).

One of the many things you'll learn from this book, and thus the art of san soo, is the ability to think for yourself in a sudden violent situation. Before you dismiss this concept as trite, consider how most martial art styles teach self-defense. In most instances you're taught a lesson. You're taught that when a person punches at you, you'll do this, that, this, that and that, and the opponent will be lying in a bloody pile at your feet.

You'll go through the lesson over and over until you have it so ingrained that your body will act of its own accord and dispense with the attacker forthwith (or so they say). In reality no two people will attack you in the same manner. Thus if you prepare for one action, you can be certain you'll get another. If you have a predetermined vision of your opponent punching, kicking, or punching and kicking simultaneously, you'll probably be tackled and beaten.

With san soo, instead of depending upon a lesson, you'll depend upon yourself. You needn't get anxious about what lesson or technique to employ as a situation progresses to violence. The anticipation of the blow is what will get you hit. Instead, relax and don't worry about it.

If you and I were playing catch with ball and glove and you're anticipating a flyball when I throw instead a fast ground ball, you'll more than likely miss it. When you anticipate something, you subconsciously prepare for that action. However, if you're simply relaxed and alert, you'll take the ball as it comes. *See everything and anticipate nothing!*

By training in san soo, you will learn to react *spontaneously*

Figure 18

to a sudden attack rather than conjure up a lesson that's not exactly pertinent to the situation. You'll think for yourself, solving your own problems as soon as you encounter them.

Solving self-defense problems with the principles of san soo is not unlike learning mathematics in school. Your teacher addresses the problem, shows you what the actual problem is, demonstrates ways to solve the problem by example, allows you to use your most valuable instrument (your mind) to solve the problem, and critiques your solution (you and your san soo partner do this for each other). If your math teacher were to give you the solutions to all the problems, you'd probably associate some problems with some solutions, but you wouldn't learn anything!

Considering all the possibilities, you will ultimately develop your own self-defense scheme far better than I or any other instructor can develop for you because only you know just how far you're willing to go to injure your attacker. Therefore, analyze your problem as it develops and solve it your way, using the tools (principles) you've acquired in your san soo training.

Chapter 2

───────

TSOI GA:
THE ART
OF STRIKING

*The amateur Kung Fu man shoots out his hands ferociously,
but lacks any true power. A Master is not so flamboyant, but
his touch is as heavy as a mountain.*

Chueh Yuan

I chose to introduce the Tsoi Ga Family of kung fu san
soo by citing the above adage. While it may not be a major
revelation, it illustrates the fact that there's more to punching
than simply punching.

Martial art Masters are not imbued with the mystical
qualities the film industry would have you believe (although
there are some who would have you believe otherwise).
Many people enter the martial arts with the hopes and
aspirations of becoming a black belt, a degreed black belt,
or even a Master. An aura of awe and mystique seems to
be synonymous with these lofty ranks, simply because they
initially appear to be far beyond immediate reach.

If you are such a person, I'll share a secret with you. *The
only thing that separates the beginner from the Master is
knowledge and the ability to make knowledge and application
intrinsic.* This is especially true with fighting—utilizing

knowledge of the mechanics of hitting with the principles of unarmed combat.

Punching and kicking play a major, if not singular, role in fighting. People who are skilled in the martial arts learn to be adept at both, but usually end up favoring one over the other. If you want to defend yourself to the best of your abilities, then it would be to your utmost advantage to be able to kick and punch spontaneously, instead of having some preconceived self-defense pattern in your head.

Most people are capable of punching or kicking well enough to pose a threat to you, even if they lack the benefits of martial training. It's important that you remember this, because if you ever take it for granted that you know how to defend yourself more effectively than your opponent knows how to defend himself, you'll underestimate him. That would be too costly a mistake for you to make even once.

Your basic punches and kicks are good weapons to have at your disposal to initiate contact in a fight should the occasion ever arise (it will). They're good follow-up tools as well, but you'll be well ahead of the game if you can launch your strike swiftly and with telling effect before your opponent realizes that he is now the victim of his own aggression.

There are punches and kicks that lend themselves better to certain situations. The choice of punch, kick, or combination of techniques is entirely your responsiblity, and only you can know what your particular situation warrants. Therefore, the better you can execute any or all of the punches, kicks, and techniques, the better you'll be able to cope with whatever you're likely to encounter.

The fighting styles of many people leave a great deal to be desired in the way of prowess. People who appear street tough, as well as a number of people you might know and presume to be formidable foes, may actually resemble kangaroos swatting at a swarm of bees when subjected to sudden violence. So, *be sudden; be violent!*

Never give your opponent the opportunity to beat you! When you can hit effectively and the time comes to attack, utilize the distance principle to your best advantage. Since you'll strike first in this context, step in close to him so that his reaction time is appreciably reduced (invade his safe distance). At this point you can do any number of things as the situation dictates. You must also bear in mind, however, that once you invade his safe distance, you will also have reduced your own. So once you decide to move in to him, BAM! Hit him immediately.

We'll go into this topic in more depth in the Fut Ga chapter, but for the moment, you should closely examine your ethics and seriously consider incorporating offense to your ideals of self-defense (if you hadn't already). Your punching, kicking, and hitting skills can be very effective when utilized in this fashion.

Before we get into the actual mechanics of different punches, I want to share a few things with you about the punching process itself. First, it's important to note that when you punch, you should refrain from making a fist until you actually hit an opponent. If you make a fist before you punch, you'll be using conflicting muscles that will inhibit your speed. On the premise that force times speed equals power, you'll want to attain the fastest punching speed as you can, as well as the most force. You derive force from the amount of weight you would put behind the blow (putting your body into it).

When you think of punching, you may have the idea of delivering a fast flurry of punches, laying on a heavy barrage of stunning blows. It's natural if you do. It's also a natural assumption to think in terms of jabbing, feinting, bobbing and weaving, and counterpunching. Great! If you're an accomplished boxer, then this is a good thing for you to do. If you aren't, I would have to advise against fighting in this way because defending yourself is not a sport, it's survival! I can't emphasize this point strongly enough.

If you were to deliver a fast flurry of punches to your opponent's head and body, you probably wouldn't be hitting with much effect if he is big and powerfully built. Why? Accuracy and power! Without hitting accurately (more on this in Chapter 6) and putting your body weight into the punches, you would not be making enough impact on him to keep him from hitting you back before you finish.

Ideally, you should hit with enough force with each blow to damage an opponent. Even though you'd be delivering fewer punches than if you dealt a flurry, you'd be hitting more accurately and powerfully and you would also be employing the pain principle to its logical and strategic advantage.

For example, if you punch to the solar plexus or up into the groin and follow up immediately with a punch to the face, such an attack would be effective. However, if you allow his body to react to your initial low punch, his head and torso will fold over and accord you better penetration and leverage to punch up into the head harder than you could if you follow up immediately.

Extended Punch

An especially good punch for you to employ for accuracy and power—should you initiate the attack or deflect an initial blow and counter—is the extended punch. An extended punch can give you a good deal of reach as well as incorporate your body weight to its maximum efficiency to stop and neutralize your opponent. More importantly, the extended punch utilizes a number of peripheral principles that are applicable to other punches, techniques, and movement skills.

To execute an extended punch, begin by standing relaxed and in a normal posture. If you're going to deliver a right punch, step forward with the right foot as you strike. Set your foot down as your punch lands, and exhale sharply as you hit. Your fist should be striking vertically and in a straight line to your target, knuckles in line with your forearm (preventing your wrist from spraining).

This should place you sideways to your opponent. Your left leg should remain stationary and locked out for this punch—this will enable you to channel your energy forward into the opponent. You're also less likely to be bowled over should he charge, and you'll offer minimal target area.

As you punch, pivot your shoulders sharply (as though drawing back a bow with your free hand) to get more speed and power from the torso. Also, try not to fully extend your arm until you make actual contact. Punch *through* him, not to him (Fig. 19).

Figure 19

Now try it with your left hand, remembering to step with the same side with which you punch. As you practice, take the time to assess your posture and position at the completion of each punch. Make sure the toes of the foot you step with are pointed at your opponent; this will enable you to gain more penetration by letting you lean further in due to the flex of your knee alignment. Make sure your head is in line with your pelvis to maintain proper center of gravity.

If you lean your head too far forward, you can be pulled off balance if your punch is deflected. Conversely, if your head is tilted too far back, you'll rob your punch of power and be subject to being pushed back and bowled over.

If you're practicing a right hand extended punch, you'll want your left hand to stop in front of your solar plexus to protect against a possible counterattack. With your protecting hand in this position, you'll be able to defend against a kick to your groin or a punch to your face. Also, be sure that your feet are in a direct line with each other so that you won't unnecessarily expose your groin or chest to attack. Don't go any further in this book until you've practiced and perfected this punch.

Backhand Punch

Now that you're back after having sweated, practiced, and ultimately mastered the extended punch, we'll move on to yet another punch that will also help you learn some of the peripheral principles of san soo.

The backhand punch is a quick, practical, and powerful punch to use either as an initial blow or counterpunch. As a first strike, you can achieve a high degree of surprise with little telegraphic movement; you may also derive a surprising amount of power with little physical exertion if you practice and achieve the correct timing.

To execute a backhand punch, begin in a relaxed posture and step in with the same foot as your punching hand. This is the same as the extended punch, only this time you'll want to bring your hands around as though swinging a baseball bat. Strike with the outside edge of your right hand, and your left will follow up with strong torque from the torso (Fig. 20).

Just as when you initiate the extended punch, you'll want to settle your weight on your leading leg as you make contact with the blow. Check to ensure you're in correct body alignment to glean the most power you possibly can without sacrificing your balance.

The significant additions to this punch worth noting are the power you'd gain through upper-body torque and

Figure 20

forward momentum, the accessibility of your hand for a
follow-up punch, and the ability to adapt the punch into an
outblock should your opponent attack at the same time as
you. You can also employ a subtle prepunch windup movement by relaxing and turning to the side (keeping your eyes
on the opponent) to gather your hands at the hip and then
striking.

A slight variation of the backhand punch can be achieved
by rapping the opponent with your knuckles instead of the
outside edge of your hand. An advantage to hitting in this
way is the quick flicking action that can generate a powerful
impact to a smaller surface area on the opponent's head
(i.e., eyes, nose, temple). Striking in this manner would be
called a back knuckles punch.

You can work on relaxing your body position and mental
attitude when you initiate this blow in order to better

facilitate speed and accuracy. Now, put this book down and practice long and hard. Don't come back and finish reading until you can effectively complete the punches as soon as you think of it. *Explode!* Your thought and punch should be simultaneous.

Roundhouse Punch

The next punch for you to practice is the roundhouse punch. The roundhouse is a highly effective way of hitting when in close to your opponent, and it allows you to hit with a great deal of force when properly executed. Your arms are closer to your body, where you'll have greater strength and leverage to put into the blow, as well as the utilization of your legs to pivot your torso quickly and efficiently into your following strikes. Your roundhouse punch can be considered the heavy artillery in your arsenal of striking methods.

To execute this punch, either stand before your heavy bag or have your partner hold a seat cushion to his chest. Unlike the extended or backhand punch, you'll be stepping in with the *opposite* foot of the hand you'll be punching with.

For a right roundhouse punch, step in and to the left of the bag and punch with your right hand as your left foot comes to rest on the floor. Resist the temptation to swing your arm into the punch; simply swing your torso into the blow. In this way, you'll be able to put the weight of your upper body into the blow for a more powerful strike.

From there you can simply pivot in the opposite direction and hit the bag with the opposite fist. For example, if you were to step in with a right roundhouse punch to the solar plexus, you could then pivot back in the opposite direction and land a left roundhouse to the kidneys.

You'll find that the closer your arms are to your body, the more power you'll have. To better illustrate what I mean, extend your arm out to the side and have your partner try to lower it while you resist. Since that is easily accomplished, try it again, only this time tuck your elbow in to your side with just your forearm extended. Much more difficult, wasn't it? So, the closer your arms are to your body, the more strength and leverage you'll have.

Now take time to practice the roundhouse punch. Remember to step in with the opposite foot, strike as your foot comes to rest, and pivot your torso into the punch instead of swinging your arm. When your feel completely comfortable with the punch, go back and practice the other ones and try to put together combinations.

These are basic and very easy punches for you to learn. Those of you who have already trained in the martial arts may consider the punches and kicks in san soo to be similar to your own. This is not necessarily so; if you look more closely at the description of the strikes, you'll note subtle—but profound—differences. The primary difference is that in san soo you initiate strikes from a relaxed, normal posture rather than a stance. Though similar in appearance to the strikes you may be using, the san soo method of striking utilizes *natural* dynamics of kinetic energy rather than straining the musculature to deliver a blow that wouldn't be as powerful.

Thus far, I've shared with you a few punches incorporating the fist to batter and bludgeon an attacker, ostensibly to injure him. But as is often the case, you must prepare for an attack from a friend, relative, or good acquaintance who's had too much to drink, or who is enraged over a real or imagined slight. In this particular instance, you should use palm strikes to various places to stop or otherwise repel his attack. I'll go into more detail on places to strike in the Hoi Ga chapter, but for now it suffices to know that you can efficiently utilize a palm strike by striking the solar plexus, temporal lobe, kidneys, or chin to name a few spots.

Palm Strike

A palm strike is versatile in that you can alter it instantly to a claw, gouge, finger jab, grab, or even a simple slap (not so simple if slapped across the nose or to the ear—ouch!). To effect a palm strike, hold out your forearm and reach the top of your hand as far back as it will go toward your wrist. You'll be hitting with the fleshy pads at the bottom of your palm, deriving the main force from the forearm (Fig. 21).

The palm strike is most often used in a thrusting manner but can also be used laterally as though in a roundhouse type movement. Either way, you'll still need to coincide your strike with your step to get maximum benefit from the blow. The step can be made with either foot as long as you can enter deeply enough to take the opponent's center of gravity when you strike.

Practice hitting in this manner until you feel comfortable with it, and then attempt to use right and left palm strikes in combinations, much as you would with a regular punch. Finally, try to incorporate palm strikes simultaneously.

Consider palm-striking to the forehead to lean your opponent's torso back, and then palm-strike with the other hand to the hip or pelvis (now more accessible due to the forehead strike). Or:

- palm-strike in and downward to his pelvis and follow up with a palm strike under the jaw (since his head will lower from the previous blow).

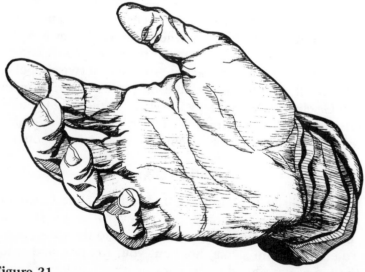

Figure 21

- palm strike with both hands to the head and follow up with a knee into the groin.
- palm strike to both lower ribs (simultaneously) as you butt your head into his face.

Problem solve; find your own combinations, set ups, and follow-up strikes, and employ them in your training so that you can move from one attack to another without being at a loss as to what to do next.

By its own definition, the Tsoi Ga family of kung fu san soo deals with the art of striking, and striking is a very personal and subjective facet of the martial arts. It should be viewed with the idea that one method of hitting is superior to another method only as it relates to the individual martial artist; no one method is universally superior to another in all situations and when used by all martial artists.

It's with this thought in mind that I point out an important aspect of striking: when we consider hitting someone, invariably we think of punching. In most instances that's all right—unless your opponent is large boned and you're small boned. For the majority of women and a number of men, punching someone in the head is a poor choice because of the disparity in density of bone mass. Small, light people will be more hurt from the blow than the person being struck because of the density of facial bone and the fragility of the bones in the hand.

The human hand is comprised of twenty-seven bones connected by tendon, ligament, muscle, nerves, blood vessels, and skin. Our hands aren't designed to be used as battering weapons, as any MD can attest to after having repaired broken and sprained fingers, knuckles, and wrists. Professional fighters know this and take appropriate measures to wrap their hands to protect them.

Compare the skeletal form of the hand with the skull in the illustrations to get a better idea of just what you're up against when you attempt to put your all into a punch to someone's face (Fig. 22a, b). In this perspective, you'd be hitting with your weaker point to an opponent's stronger

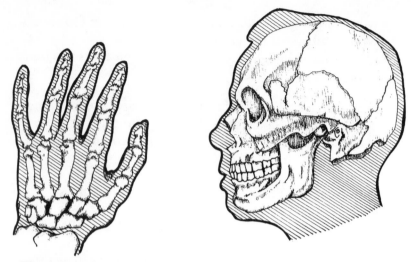

Figure 22a,b

point (hand to head). In order to reverse roles and hit with a stronger (more bone mass) to a weaker area, consider hitting with the forearm and the juncture of the wrist (Fig. 22c). Bone density is thicker nearest the wrist and you can incorporate a hammering blow with this area that will maximize your hitting potential.

The bones of the forearm are the radius and the ulna; you should strike with the ulna at and slightly above the wrist

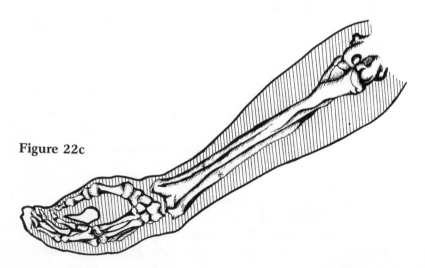

Figure 22c

as indicated in the illustration. Though the bone is actually thicker in the radius portion of the forearm, the strength and thickness of the lower ulna is more than sufficient to meet your hitting needs.

In striking with the forearm, you can effectively break the clavicle (collarbone), injure the cervical vertebrae at the base of the skull, break facial bones, or deliver a blow painful enough to achieve a charley horse effect to any muscular area. Note that all of these strikes are aimed at more fragile bones or softer muscle—were you to hit thick, hard bone (as in the top of the skull, knee, or shin), you'd be in nearly as much pain as your opponent.

Striking with the forearm also has an advantage in that—because of its length—you can hit more than one vulnerable area with one blow. You can strike to the side of the neck and hit the external jugular vein and the carotid artery; a strike to the back of the head will hit the cervical vertebrae and the cerebellum, and a strike to the juncture of any joint will injure and impair mobility of the limb.

Now, after you've explored and practiced the many ways to incorporate the strikes you've learned thus far, including using them in combination with each other, consider the grim prospect of not being able to use any of your limbs to assist you in the event of an attack.

Visualize yourself walking down a sidewalk. It's early evening and not very many people are out; you're on your way to a department store to purchase an item of clothing, cologne, or whatever you think you need to make a favorable impression on your date this night.

A smile begins to play across your face as you envision your date later in the evening, extolling your prowess in the ways of love as you feign modesty. At this point, while lost in reverie, a man steps in front of you and grabs you in a bear hug. Your arms are pinned to your sides and you don't have the leg clearance to knee him. He begins to squeeze the breath out of you as he moves you into an alleyway to do God only knows what. What will you do?

Struggle as you might, you still can't manage to gain

enough clearance to punch or knee him. As your last conscious breath begins to fade away, you finally start to use your head. You bite his face or ear to make him tilt his head back so that you can smash your forehead repeatedly into his face until he releases you. Then you can extract whatever punishment on him that you decide.

Silly little scenario, wasn't it? Be that as it may, I now have you seriously considering adding head butts into your repertoire of striking methods. (In a curious way, people tend to bypass the things in life that are too easy or readily accessible, figuring all the while that because something is quick and easy, it lacks merit.)

Head Butt

Using a head butt is quick and easy and is a superior method of striking an opponent when in close; that's a fact. A head butt strike is equally effective as an initial blow or as a defensive strike when inside an opponent's circles of influence.

When utilizing a head butt, strike with the frontal portion of your skull. This section accords you sufficient bone density to effect a powerful impact to the weaker facial bones, cartilage, mandibular joints, and teeth as well as the opponent's vulnerable temporal lobes. *Do not* head-butt your opponent forehead to forehead as is done by rams on various wildlife television programs; the reason is obvious, although I must admit to wanting to watch someone try it!

A head butt can be especially effective when stepping between your opponent's feet to take his center of gravity as you pin his arms to his sides (Fig. 23). You can then incorporate this strike to smash directly into his face, or you can strike from one side of his head to the other by smashing with your head as you pull his torso from side to side for added impact.

When grabbed from behind, a head butt using the back of the head is an excellent first strike while you effect your release. The back of the head (occipital faction of the skull, below the lambdoidal suture) can be utilized as an uppercut

Figure 23

type of blow very efficiently when infighting. When you work out with your partner, explore these possibilities.

Biting

Let's now look at a facet of violence that may seem a tad unsavory to some of you: biting. I'm not talking about biting just hard enough to make someone yell; I'm talking about taking a dinner-sized chunk. It all comes back to causing enough pain to disable an attacker. If you bite someone just hard enough to let you go, you'll really be in for some trouble unless you follow through immediately. If you bite off the end of a man's nose, however, he'll be more concerned with his own pain than he will be with attacking you again.

When most people bite, more often than not they will take too big of a bite. If you open your mouth as wide as you can to take a bite out of an apple, you'll realize that you need to take a smaller bite for better leverage; this is also true when you bite a person.

Have you ever watched a dog bite into something? It doesn't simply clamp its teeth down on whatever (or whoever) it's biting, but shakes its head violently to rip and tear as well. So if you're going to seriously bite someone, take a small bit for better leverage and shake your head to assist your teeth in its ripping and tearing (barking and growling is optional).

A word of caution: biting is designed to cause intensive pain and trauma, and it is likely that you will draw blood. In this day and age you run the risk of contracting AIDS if your opponent has the AIDS virus in his system (and he does not have to be gay to have it). This is particularly true if you already have a mouth injury.

Gouging and Clawing

Gouging and clawing are right up there with biting to elicit a high pain response. Gouging and clawing are exceptionally fine techniques at your disposal when engaged in close infighting. In order to best gouge and claw, you'll want to keep your fingers rigid. Instead of simply raking the fingers across the face to scratch, you should first punch *in* with your hand held as a claw and then gouge and tear downward or to the side. There are highly sensitive nerve endings in the face which make this type of blow painful indeed. And again, as with any kind of blow, you should follow through with another to buy you time to put him away or flee.

You can incorporate gouging and clawing with biting at the same time, or follow one with another, depending upon your relative position to your opponent. You can effectively bite into the nose, throat, carotid artery, ears, or any place you can lock onto while you do damage with your hands.

Knee and Elbow Strikes

Knee and elbow strikes are pretty much self-explanatory, but if you're the least bit creative, you can find many ways to use them. We'll explore a few possibilities here.

To begin with, you can use your knee to strike horizontally into the solar plexus, ribs, groin, or thighs (Fig. 24). Once you avoid an opponent's punch or kick, you can grab his clothing or part of his body to pull him in to you as you slam your knee across. If you step deep enough past the attacker so that you're facing his back, you can knee horizontally into the spine or kidneys.

Another way to utilize your knee strikes would be to strike vertically. You can pull your attacker's head down and knee up into the face (Fig. 25), solar plexus, and groin. Keep in mind that if you knee him once, you can knee him a dozen times in rapid succession, not unlike running in place into the groin or solar plexus. This is an especially good way to deal with someone who tries to get you in a clinch or bear hug.

Another way to incorporate a vertical knee would be to use it as a stationary object and pull the opponent down onto it. For instance, you can get past the opponent's attack and pull his head down by the hair onto your knee (Fig. 26). You can also pull him down from behind so that his back (spine) is dropped onto your knee. This technique can be done from a standing position as well (Fig. 27).

Figure 24

Figure 25

Figure 26

Figure 27

Elbow strikes are often more powerful weapons than fists—because the closer to your body, the more power you have. You can utilize a downward elbow strike by folding the opponent over and striking down to the spine, kidneys, or back of the head or neck (Fig. 28). You can also straighten his arm out once you've neutralized him to strike down behind his elbow to break his arm.

Striking with the elbow horizontally is also a highly efficient technique. You can hit with a great deal of force into the face, throat, ribs, or solar plexus (Fig. 29). Hitting in this way is a good offensive move once you decide to initiate the attack. Used as a counterattack, you can duck under a punch and slam his lower ribs to buckle him, then follow up with a knee strike to the head. There are endless opportunities to use elbows and knees for close fighting and many possible combinations for use in conjunction with punching and kicking techniques.

When approached from behind or after having gotten past your opponent, you can incorporate a backward elbow strike to hurt him (Fig. 30). Hitting in this way is especially useful when defending yourself in close quarters where there is little room to punch or kick.

Another way of using elbow strikes is as an uppercut. In this fashion you can hit up into the chin or groin with a great deal of power and lift (Fig. 31). You can step between the opponent's legs and uppercut into the jaw or throat, depending upon the situation.

When you deliver any of the elbow strikes, be attentive that you are in fact hitting with the elbow and not the forearm or upper arm, as is often the case. Spend some time working out, using nothing but knees and elbows to defend yourself with. Work out in slow motion when you do this so that you'll hit accurately and in good position.

Let's move on now to the subject of kicking. It seems that in most instances, kung fu and karate are synonymous with kicking, and I'm not going to disappoint you by saying otherwise. We often see martial artists in movies and magazines kicking someone's head with long reaching legs. Awesome!

Figure 28

Figure 29

Figure 30

Figure 31

Pretty to look at, fun to watch. But unless you have an excellent stretch to your legs, I suggest you set your sights a little lower. Why? Because by the time the leg is extended to the head, much of the power and penetration will have dissipated.

If, however, you already happen to be a superb kicker, then by all means kick wherever you like. Most people could kick to the head if they really tried, but unless you're well trained, it wouldn't be a very effective blow.

As you may or may not be aware, you have a much longer reach with your legs than with your arms; you also have more strength in your legs than in your arms. You can kick with a great deal of accuracy if you think of your knee as something akin to a rifle sight; wherever you point your knee, your foot will follow (Fig. 32).

Whenever you opt to kick rather than punch, resist the temptation of straight-legging it. Try instead to throw your knee into it for more snap and impact. Don't confuse this as a cocking motion preceding a kick; cocking a kick or punch takes time and is too obvious to a streetwise opponent. If you kick with a straight leg, you'll risk the chance of your opponent capturing it—and you won't like the consequences.

Your choice of a particular kick in a self-defense situation depends upon how much or how little actual damage you want to administer. Other things to consider when you kick are your relative position to an opponent, the kind of footing you do or don't have, whether the opponent is standing or charging, and the type of clothing you and your opponent have on (jeans, swim trunks, ski pants, hip waders, etc.).

There are a wide variety of kicks taught in kung fu san soo; in this book, though, I'll confine myself to the kicks that the average person should be able to accomplish without personal instruction.

Snap Kick

A good basic kick for you to begin with that you'll probably use first, should you ever need to kick, is called a snap kick. The snap kick enables you to attack an opponent's vital

Figure 32

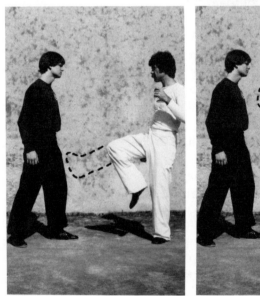

frontal areas; in particular the groin, knees, shins, solar plexus or head (if you feel you have the reach and power).

Begin from a relaxed posture. For a right snap kick, shift the balance of your weight onto your left foot and pivot on the ball of that foot as you snap your right leg out to kick

Figure 33

directly in front of you (Fig. 33). You can strike with the ball of your foot, heel, or the whole bottom of your foot.

When you execute this kick, be sure to pivot sideways to the opponent to attain maximum reach, penetration, and power from the hips, offering the opponent very little target area. Have your hands up and ready for punching if you aren't going to kick him again. You can, however, punch and kick at the same time. If you choose to do so, it's usually best to punch with the same side as you kick. Practice the snap kick until you can deliver it as fast as you can without telegraphing your intent.

Strive to become as adept with your left kicks as you are with your right. Once you feel you can execute this and the following kicks to your satisfaction, try using them in combinations. This doesn't mean you should feel compelled to use a combination of kicks simply because you can do them well; at times it may become more expedient to use hand techniques. When you've learned to be proficient with your hands, feet, knees, elbows, and head and can use them in combination with each other, you'll have more striking tools to hit an opponent with than he will have; so in a sense, he'll be outnumbered by you.

Roundhouse Kick

The next kick for you to practice is a roundhouse kick, which is effective in many situations. However, the kick will lose some of its destructive impact if it's launched at less than a perpendicular angle to an opponent's body—in other words, you want to avoid a glancing kick.

The roundhouse kick can be instrumental in either initiating an attack or fending one off. If you wish to stun an opponent rather than injure him, you can kick with the instep to the lower ribs or to the side of the knee to buckle him. You can also kick to his outer thigh with your shin to temporarily paralyze his leg, and then either press the attack or flee.

The applications of the roundhouse kick are as varied as the other kicks after you become familiar with it. To execute a good roundhouse, you may find it easier in the beginning to take a step as you kick. Later on when you feel more comfortable with it, try the kick from a relaxed posture.

If you're going to kick with the right leg, step forward with the left foot. Now bring your right leg up and around so that your leg and foot are parallel to the ground, as though you're kicking over a chair. Pivot sharply on the ball of your left foot, and throw your torso and knee into it. This is an all-or-nothing kind of kick, so put everything you have into it. For a left roundhouse kick, simply reverse the procedure for a right kick (Fig. 34).

You can strike using the ball of your foot, instep, or shin, depending upon where you want to hit your opponent. When using the shin as a striking surface, strike to a muscular area and not to bone (i.e., shin to thigh, shin to side of knee, or shin to the side of the rib cage). If you do strike like this, you'll be in as much pain as your opponent. opponent.

If you watch professional karate bouts, you'll see the competitors use roundhouse kicks frequently. They'll deliver

Figure 34

several in quick succession with a follow-up kick or hand technique. For them, it may be a good idea to incorporate roundhouse kicks as feints; for you, it won't be such a good idea. Why? Because the basic premise of the art of san soo is sudden violence! In a violent encounter with an opponent, you won't have time to plot stratagems like you've seen on television or in the movies or that are in your fantasies!

With this thought in mind, you would do well to consider each and every blow you deliver as heavy artillery. It's imperative that you make each punch or kick hurt or injure so that you won't be subjected to potential counterpunches and kicks by your opponent.

Side Kick

After you've practiced and become proficient with the roundhouse kick, it'll be time to move on to the side kick. There are actually two types of side kicks; the side kick and the side kick thrust. We'll start with the side kick first.

This type of kick can be utilized to deflect or stop a punch, kick the chin, kick up into the throat if you have the reach, or to kick in any number of ways you feel you can effectively do so. You may strike with the outside edge of the foot as well as the bottom and ball of your foot. For learning purposes, however, stick to using the outside (or "knife edge") of your foot.

To execute a side kick, begin from a relaxed posture. Now shift your weight to pivot on your left foot and kick upward in front of you with the right foot. This will be similar to the snap kick, only you're striking with a different angle and area of your foot. When executing a snap kick, your foot is vertical, but with a side kick the foot is held horizontal to the ground.

As with the snap kick, you'll want your hands in position to ward off any attack or counterattack from your opponent. If you're kicking with your right foot, your right hand should be held by your waist and your left hand positioned by your head, because these are the areas you most need to protect. This is merely a suggestion; if you feel more comfortable holding your hands up in a different fashion, do so.

Side Kick Thrust

The next kick for you to practice is the side kick thrust, which will give you good penetration into the solar plexus, knee, groin, or throat. You can apply this kick in an offensive or defensive manner with equal success. For instance, it can be used to stop an opponent's forward movement and give you time to counterattack.

The side kick thrust is a little bit more involved than the

side kick. You may take a step with this kick but it isn't always necessary. To begin, pivot on your left foot as you throw your right knee up into the kick, turning your body sideways and keeping your leg in line with your torso. The foot is then brought directly up and into the opponent. The force of this kick is directed straight into the opponent rather than upward as with the side kick (Fig. 35).

Figure 35

Most students practicing the side kick thrust tend to bring the leg around, as in a roundhouse kick. Try to avoid this syndrome by watching your kick in motion. Imagine there's a wall pressed in close on both sides of your body, thereby making it impossible to get a roundhouse effect into your kick. With these imaginary walls in place as a guideline, lean back slightly as you raise your knee and all at once sharply pivot your body sideways, launching your foot up and in to the opponent (not around and in).

Proper timing is necessary for this type of kick. If you lean back before you actually kick the man, you may just push yourself away from him.

In some styles of karate, the emphasis on kicks is to keep the torso upright at all times. This is fine; the kick will still work, but you'll have much more power and reach if you lean your torso, keeping it in a straight line with your leg.

To prove this, have your partner hold a kicking bag or a cushion of some kind at your belly. With your torso erect, extend your leg as far as you can so that your foot is just touching the cushion, as in a side kick thrust (so that each time you kick at it you can barely reach it). Now lean your torso back as you kick the cushion. See the difference (Fig. 36)?

Try not to make the common mistake of leaning too far back. To emphasize the proper torso position when you kick, first lean your body into it to establish your center of gravity (pelvis) *forward* of your standing leg. This will help ensure that you won't be propelling yourself away from an opponent rather than in to him. Now take this time to practice and perfect this kick.

Hopping Side Kick Thrust

The next kick, the hopping side kick thrust, will require a bit more practice and a higher degree of timing, but it will be worth it. This will be a variation of the side kick thrust, and will incorporate a short hop into the kicking motion that will apply body weight and therefore more power. This variation can be a valuable addition to your arsenal of kicks.

Figure 36

A hopping side kick thrust can be effectively employed to close the distance between yourself and an attacker to neutralize his advance. You can also incorporate this kick as a follow-up to stun or knock an opponent down after your initial attack. In time, you will discover other ways to apply this kick.

To execute this kick, step forward with the right leg if you intend to kick with the right leg. Spring yourself up with the right leg and hop with your left foot to where your right foot was. Now kick with your right leg as you settle your weight onto your left leg (Fig. 37).

Actually this is easier than it sounds. Just study the illustration and remember to kick at the same instant as your left foot sets to the ground; in this way your entire body weight drops into the kick. If all you do is hop to the left foot and then kick after your weight has settled, you'll only be kicking with the weight of your leg.

Figure 37

Spinning Kick

I'll digress for a moment to say a few words about the next kick for you to learn. This is a kick that martial artists everywhere seem to be particularly enamored with. It is difficult to really get down, and yet it is one of the most dramatic and esthetic of all the kicks. The kick I'm referring to, the kick that captivates moviegoers everywhere, is the spinning kick. There are two variations of this kick: the simple spinning kick and the leaping spinning kick. The former is what we'll concern ourselves with first.

To properly address the actual application of spinning kicks, you should know that there are further variations of this movement. The variations go under a heading all their own, and are uniquely adapted to spinning movements. These kicks are the crescent/spinning crescent, sweep/spinning sweeps, hooks/spinning hooks, and back kick/spinning back kick.

Crescent kicks, hooking kicks, and spinning kicks will require a certain degree of balance, suppleness, and coordination. Though the spinning and hook kicks are pretty much self-explanatory, I'll elaborate anyway.

A spinning kick is one in which you face an opponent and spin your body completely around, hitting him with the back of your foot. You can generate a great deal of power with this kick due to torque of the upper body and the centrifugal force of the leg sweeping around.

The hook kick is as the name implies; you face the opponent sideways or frontally and hook your leg into him with the back of your leg or foot, not unlike the final movement of a spinning kick.

Of the two, the spinning kick can generate the most power because of the momentum and body torque. There are elements involved in both these kicks, however, that are essential to generate the highest degree of power. These include correct balance, timing, pivoting, speed, and execution.

Now, prepare to execute a left spinning kick by standing in a relaxed posture facing an imaginary opponent (Fig. 38a).

Figure 38a

Figure 38b

Figure 38c

Figure 38d

Step your right foot slightly forward and to the right of your left foot so that your right heel is pointed toward the opponent (Fig. 38b). Then pivot your trunk around to the left so that you're now looking over your left shoulder at the opponent; your right heel should still be pointed toward the opponent (Fig. 38c). At this point you launch your kick, torquing your torso to the left by throwing your arms (formerly relaxed at your sides) sharply enough to have the momentum to propel your kick completely around and into your opponent (Fig. 38d).

Once you've read the text and looked at the figures sufficiently to undertake the kick, you'll probably find yourself performing the mechanics of the three steps outlined above. When you are ready, attempt to execute the kick as one continuous movement. When you're able to do it to your satisfaction, concentrate your attention on not displaying telegraphic movements such as sweeping your arms up and around.

When you connect with a spinning kick, you may either hit with your leg extended or slightly bent, or by hooking into the opponent; try all three ways. When you actually make contact, you can strike with the bottom of your foot, the heel, or even the knife edge if you choose to spin and launch your kick *through* the opponent (in much the same way as a side kick thrust).

In most traditional styles, you'll see the spinning kick executed differently than in san soo in that other practitioners will take a longer step and spin around with their arms extended throughout the course of the kick. While the spinning kick can be effectively delivered in this manner, we refrain from using it primarily because we are a street-fighting art; the longer step and splayed arms telegraph too much and therefore the kick can be aborted too readily by a streetwise opponent. And street fighting differs from sport; should we attempt to deliver a whirling, pretty spinning kick and get intercepted, a referee won't save us. Think about it.

Crescent Kick

Another popular kick with martial artists everywhere is

the crescent kick, which has some interesting variations to it worth exploring, not the least of which is the spinning crescent. But before you attempt that, begin with a simple standing crescent kick, which can be quicker and more formidable.

The crescent kick is as the name describes; the power and force of the kick are delivered in a crescent-shaped arc directly in front of you. You thrust your knee upwards and snap your lower leg in a tight arc (no wider than the width of your opponent) up and to the side, with the force of the blow reaching a peak at your planned point of impact. This should be a very fast, tight, and snapping kind of kick.

The standing crescent kick can be employed as an initial blow to the head (if you have the stretch and reach) or as a defensive blow to an arm delivering a punch or swinging a weapon. The secret to executing a powerful crescent kick is in the tight upward crescent—kick no wider than the width of your target's trunk, whether it's a kick launched from the outside inward or from the inside outward.

Most traditional styles make a deadly mistake in trying to accomplish a fast upward circle with the leg locked out because it looks prettier. While it may indeed be prettier to watch, the increased danger of getting your leg caught by the opponent isn't worth the risk. If you are in a sparring scenario or simply joking around with your friends, it wouldn't matter a whole lot what you do; but then, that isn't why you chose to explore san soo, is it?

Because san soo is entirely street oriented, the frivolous and superfluous movements of sport and traditional styles have no place, because they aren't movement effective. The following photographs will give you a better view of this (Figs. 39a & b). Figure 39a shows vulnerability to being jammed or blocked when kicking well outside the body frame (note the kick's circular path). Figure 39b shows that kicking in an upward arc (in an oval path) lessens your opponent's reaction time to your kick because of speedier delivery and less telegraphic movement.

Figure 39a

Figure 39b

Combination Kicks and Spontaneity

After you feel comfortable with the crescent kick, take the time to put together a rapid combination of punches and kicks that will flow well with each other. For a few ideas, you might try a right backhand punch as you execute a right spinning kick so that your punch and kick arrive at the same time. Try a right snap kick/right extended punch. Try a right crescent kick (clockwise) and proceed into a right spin kick.

The possibilities are truly limitless, but do explore them with both right and left strikes, striking with two different blows at once, and a series of blows in succession. The time you spend doing this now will reward you later on in your training, not so much that you actually can do them, but so that, with your familiarity of them, you'll be able to put combinations together spontaneously!

Spontaneity is truly the essence of being able to defend yourself with any degree of surety. At any given moment, no matter where you are, what you're doing, or what position you're in, you are vulnerable to a sudden attack. It's possible for you to be attacked while at a family gathering, social function, business meeting, or even while attending church. In your mind you might agree but still not be able to visualize it happening to you, and it is this that makes you all the more vulnerable to a sudden physical attack!

Seriously consider for a moment just how vulnerable you are in various situations: seated in a public restroom, restaurant, or behind the wheel of your car at a stoplight (doors unlocked); sitting, kneeling, or lying down in a park or on a sandy beach; holding a child in your arms; and getting into or out of your car or home (think back to a time when you opened your door to leave home and were startled at seeing someone about to knock, and how nervous it made you feel).

The list of places and situations are lengthy; take a few moments to list as many places as you can think of where you would be most vulnerable. After all, if you were a mugger or rapist, wouldn't you pick a victim who is least able to offer even minimal resistance? Of course you would!

Kicking from the Ground

This brings us to the next portion of your training in san soo—learning to kick from the ground. As you'll see, it is possible to deal some powerful blows from what is generally believed to be a vulnerable position (it should be noted, however, that if you're sitting or lying down and suspect you may have to defend yourself, you should stand).

For a brief exercise in executing various kicks, begin by kneeling on the floor, facing your partner. The first one to try will be a snap kick. Raise up on your left knee and kick out with your right leg in the same fashion as a standing snap kick, striking with the ball of your foot, heel, or bottom of the foot. Have your hands up and ready to deal with any punches as you kick (Fig. 40).

The kneeling snap kick is very effective in defending against a frontal assault. You can employ a kneeling snap kick to stop an opponent as he starts to attack you, or you can use it as a lead and follow through with another kick.

After practicing the snap kicks and the following kicks, you and your partner should take turns standing in front of each other, pretending to be the attacker. Then practice directing your kicks to the ankles, shins, knees, side of knees, groin, and tailbone. If you kick any higher than the waist from a kneeling position, your leg will be extended too far and you'll lack sufficient power to injure your opponent.

The next kick for you to try from a kneeling position is the side kick. This is accomplished by placing your hands on the ground at your left knee, and kicking to the right with the right leg (Fig. 41). This is a thrusting kick, and you may also utilize it against a frontal assault by pivoting on your left knee so that your kicking leg is in a direct line with your attacker.

The side kick can be employed against an attacker approaching from the side when you don't have time to face him or from the front when you do. You can hit with the knife edge, the heel, or the bottom of your foot.

Have your partner approach you as though he were going to attack. As he comes within striking range, kick lightly

Figure 40

Figure 41

to the knee nearest you. Your partner should feel how easy it would be to have his leg broken had you kicked with any degree of power. Then, as with a snap kick, have your partner stand within striking range and practice kicking his vulnerable points. It will then be your turn to stand and be kicked.

Another kick to be employed from the ground is a roundhouse kick. Drop your hands to your left side to support your upper body, then pivot on your left knee and kick horizontally to the front with your right leg (Fig. 42).

You can strike with your instep, shin, or ball of your foot. Kick to the side of the opponent's nearest leg, paying particular attention to the side of the knee to buckle him, strike with your shin to the outside of the thigh to numb and neutralize, or go for the ankle. If you kick his ankle, you can follow through with enough force to effect a sweep.

The roundhouse kick is effective against someone who is facing or approaching you with ill intent. You should practice this kick so that you are proficient with either leg and can deliver with authority at a moment's notice.

The final kick for you to practice from the floor is a back kick. You can employ a back kick against someone approaching from behind, and you would kick with the bottom of your foot or the heel. To do this kick, put your hands on the ground in front of you and look back under your right arm as you kick directly behind you with your right leg (Fig. 43). Look back under your left arm for a left back kick. From your position on the ground, it will be a simple matter of shifting your body to throw a side kick instead of a back kick if you prefer.

Once you feel you have the mechanics of these kicks down, practice kicking both legs and begin to use them in combinations in case of multiple attack. For example, in the event you're approached from the front and behind, you can snap-kick to the front and back-kick behind. If attacked from the front and the side, you can sweep the side attacker with a roundhouse kick and carry the momentum forward to pivot around and back-kick with your other leg. The

Figure 42

Figure 43

effectiveness of these counterattacks depends upon who is closest to you and how well you've practiced your kicks.

These are only a couple of examples; I want you to think for yourself and do some problem solving with your partner so that what you come up with at the moment will be completely spontaneous. Experiment with the various kicks and see how many possibilities you can come up with, list them, then throw them away. Actually doing the combinations is more important than memorizing and performing them as a lesson.

The Tsoi Ga family of kung fu san soo addresses itself primarily with the art of striking, both as an initial strike and a defensive blow. In san soo, a block or evasion will be a strike unto itself or will lead to a strike (or a series of strikes) to fully incapacitate an opponent.

But before we continue along these lines, I'd like to remind you that a block or evasion wouldn't be necessary if you attack your opponent in the very instant you realize a fight is imminent!

There will be a time, however, when you're attacked by someone who'll give you no indication of his aggressive intentions. This is where you will need to incorporate blocks and evasions.

Outgrab

A simple and very effective means of dealing with a punch already launched is called an outgrab. With an outgrab, you can yank an opponent into a punch or kick, pull him off balance, or guide his punch to either side of you to open up different areas of his body. Although this particular method of deflection is best employed against jabs, it can also be effectively used against hooking or roundhouse types of punches.

In order to best utilize an outgrab, you must keep your wrist relaxed and supple. Have your partner extend his arm as though he were punching at you; the idea is to hook his punch past you. As soon as you make contact with his arm, let your wrist and hand drape over his wrist so as to pull him off balance or to direct his punch to the side. (Fig. 44).

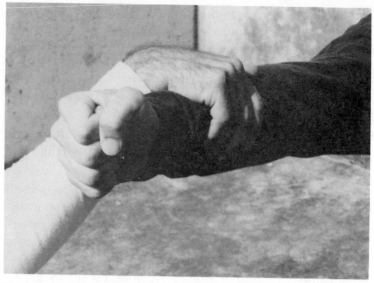

Figure 44

It's important for you to not actually grab the wrist because of the possibility of injuring your thumb. You want to capture his arm just enough to pull him past or to apply a leverage technique; just think in terms of hooking him past rather than clutching.

Experiment with the many ways you can apply an outgrab. You might consider pulling him into your punch, elbow, or kick. You can hook him past you as you knee him in the groin or solar plexus. At times, you can outgrab him hard enough and with enough momentum to effect a takedown.

Windmill Block

Another type of deflective block is called a windmill. This method involves sweeping your arm in an arc that carries the blow aside to expose his frontal target areas or back, depending upon which windmill direction you employ (Fig. 45). Generally you sweep his punch downward and to the side, but you may also sweep it upward and to the side with equal success if you want to expose his rib cage.

Begin practicing the windmill by having your partner

Figure 45

throw a right punch to your face. Launch your block when you detect the initial movement of the upper arm he's punching with. As soon as you make contact with his arm, let your wrist and hand drape over his wrist to deflect and pull him off balance or to direct the punch to the side in much the same way as an outgrab. Then swing his arm down and to your right. This will expose his right rib cage as well as his kidneys to you. Pivot sideways as you utilize the windmill to present less target area on yourself.

If your partner delivers a left punch, do exactly the same thing. This will expose his frontal areas to you if you're still using your right arm.

Don't forget to move in on him and attack! You haven't hurt him as yet, and he can still attack you. As soon as you get his punch out of the way, deal with him as the situation dictates. You and your partner should practice the windmill with each arm equally. Have your partner deliver some combination punches—if all goes well, you'll be far into your own attack before his first one lands, thereby aborting any follow-up strikes he may have intended.

It is important to keep your elbows tucked in close to your

body so you won't be tempted to reach for his punching hand (after all, your opponent will bring it to you soon enough). If you reach for him, you'll minimize the effectiveness of this deflection by committing your limb to an action that your opponent could take advantage of. The windmill is also a very effective means of defending against kicks if you're just within kicking range.

Crossblock

The next method of deflection is a power block. It's called a crossblock because you cross your body to power-strike his hitting arm forcefully enough to upset his balance. You can utilize a crossblock quickly and easily to block a punch or kick and then inflict an injury, to disarm a weapon, to knock an opponent off balance as an initial strike, or even as a follow-up power blow sufficient to break bones.

To better get the feel of a crossblock, have your partner deliver you a right punch and hold it there. With his arm extended, step into the middle of him with your right leg and immediately pivot to your left to strike his arm with your right forearm (Fig. 46). You can: hit with the muscle

Figure 46

of your forearm to stun and knock him away from you, hit with the lower bone of your forearm (ulna) to a muscle area to temporarily paralyze, or hit to smaller bones to break them (i.e., collar, wrist, neck, etc.).

When you've stepped into him, you will want to settle into what is called a full horse position. This stance will give you a sufficient balance point from which to direct your strike without being moved off balance yourself. For easy reference, see Figure 47 and use these positions to better facilitate moving and striking techniques.

This will be as close as you will ever come in san soo to employing a stance of any kind. Even at that, the only reason you would utilize one of these positions would be to launch an attack of some kind. You will not be required to hold the full or half horse position for lengthy periods, just long enough to accomplish whatever action you're going to take.

Let's return to the crossblock now. When your partner throws a punch at you, strike his forearm as hard as you can with your forearm (muscle) to knock it out of the way. Having done this a few times, switch roles. This will be uncomfortable but shouldn't cause any injury.

Now switch again so that you're going to block his arm. This time when you block him, instead of striking entirely with your arm, extend your right arm to your right side parallel to the ground and bend your elbow so that your fist is at your head level. Now step in to him and pivot at the waist so that you're putting your torso and waist into the block. Don't just hit with your arm—move your upper body sharply to carry out the strike (Fig. 48). You should be able to notice the significant increase in force you're now able to put into the block; your partner should, too.

As a precaution, keep your left hand up to protect your face in case you strike him on the inside of the elbow. This will cause his arm to bend at the elbow and his fist to hit you in the face if you aren't prepared.

Once you've practiced the crossblock, it can be used very effectively to defend against jabs, roundhouse punches, and even kicks if you get to the inside and strike above the knee.

Figure 47: Full-horse and half-horse stance.

Figure 48

Outblock

The next type of blocking method is called the outblock, which is simple, direct, and very efficient. The outblock can be used to block the same types of attacks as the crossblock, and it can also be used to attack simultaneously with your opponent.

The mechanics of the outblock are much the same as those of the backhand punch. Begin by having your partner deliver you a right punch. Step in to him and block to the left with your left forearm as you bring your right hand up to protect and add momentum to the block. You may step in to him with either foot, but for now step in with your left foot. It should turn out so that you're able to punch with your right hand at the same time as your left forearm knocks his blow aside (Fig. 49).

Other Deflecting Techniques

You should keep in mind that you can execute any of these blocks or deflections regardless of which hand your attacker punches with. You shouldn't even have to change positions; their very nature is such that they alter the opponent's position instead of your own. If you've established your distance correctly and read the opponent's body English well enough, you should be able to swat his blow aside as you step into or alongside him (Fig. 50).

Other methods of deflection that you should consider include, outgrabbing with one hand and punching with the other, kicking at the same time as you block, and spitting full in your opponent's face as you block. You may also deliver a good block with a rolling motion—slapping his punch downward and to the side with your right hand, continue leading it past with your left, and delivering a strong backhand punch with your right. This motion is not unlike the gestures you would make while playing patty-cake with a small child (I know that sounds silly, but it's *very* effective).

Keep in mind the fact that blocking a blow is only one part of the whole picture. If you simply ward off a punch or kick, you can bet you're going to have to do it again and again. You will do well to gear yourself to immediately follow up your block with an attack of your own.

Ideally, if you think your opponent is going to attack you with a combination of punches, he should be struck hard before his first punch is fully launched, and harder yet before his second punch has even become an idea in his head; this way you won't be stepping into a flurry of punches. If you

Figure 49

Figure 50

don't attack before he does, attack as he does.

Some of these movements may seem foreign to you. Indeed you may even want to skip any or all of them entirely; hang in there. If you practice these movements as you should, handling an attack will be as natural as breathing.

Defending Against Kicks

In practically any street-fight situation, you'll have to defend yourself from a simple kick to a variety of kicks, depending upon your opponent's experience. In this last segment of utilizing the Tsoi Ga principles of san soo, you will be acquainted with a method of deflecting these kicks to put yourself in position to neutralize and strike your attacker.

You should bear in mind, however, that if the man attacking you is truly proficient in his kicking ability and you haven't correctly read his body English or applied the principles of line, distance, angle, and movement, you will be hit. Protecting yourself is your responsibility, not mine or anyone else who attempts to teach you. In this light, I again stress the importance of practicing the techniques and principles of san soo long and hard.

It will be to your decided advantage to be able to kick as well or better than anyone you're likely to encounter. In addition to the people who are adept at kicking, the popularity of martial art films has produced a number of people who have no previous training in the arts, but who can deliver kicks as readily and almost as well as the screen hero, merely by mimicry.

Kicking is an art within itself; indeed there are martial art styles that deal almost exclusively with kicking. But you should know that while kicking is a powerful tool for the right person, it's only a small part in the total arsenal of body weapons san soo practitioners have at their disposal. My reason for mentioning this is twofold; first, I want you to be very aware of the power and effectiveness of kicking. Second, I don't want you to be unnecessarily frightened of having to deal with a kick.

Perhaps the most common kick you'll have to deal with is something similar to a snap kick that resembles someone kicking a football; this will normally be followed by a series of punches. A kick of this type can be quite sudden and executed without too much telegraphic movement.

A good sense of timing is as valuable an asset as reading your opponent's body English to successfully defend yourself from a snap kick. This being the case, you and your partner should pay particular attention to developing your sense of timing by defending against ever-accelerating kicks until you reach full speed.

The first technique for you to try will be instrumental in dealing with a variety of kicks in addition to the snap kick.

First establish your safe distance, and then have your partner direct a snap kick to your midsection. At the initial movement of his upper thigh to lift and deliver the kick, lift your knee sharply to neutralize the kick before it's fully delivered. You can also deflect with your shin or the side of your knee if the kick has already been launched (Fig. 51). You can do this by bringing your knee either directly up or swinging it sharply to the side to knock his kick aside.

In addition to the obvious advantages of this technique, you'll be protecting your groin when you lift your knee, as well as setting yourself up to retaliate with a return kick of your own wherever there's an opening. For example, you'll be in a good position to kick his standing leg at the side of the knee to take him down.

Another defense against a snap kick would be to step in to the attacker as you strike his leg with the top of your forearm to deflect the kick (Fig. 52). Your forearm should be vertical and swung to the side to deflect the kick. Strike with the top of your forearm rather than the bottom in this instance because there is a strong chance the force of the kick would straighten your arm suddenly enough to break it. If you intend to block with your right arm, you should step in with your right leg to offer less of yourself as a target area in case your timing is off and you miss your block. If you step in with the same leg as the arm you block with,

Figure 51

Figure 52

you'll be able to block either leg he kicks with. The only difference in the effect will be that he'll have different vulnerable areas exposed to you, depending upon which leg he kicks with. For example, if he kicks with the right leg and you step in to him with your right leg and block with the right arm, you'll have his frontal areas exposed to you. If he kicks with his left leg and you block him again with your right arm (and right step) in the same direction, you'll have his back and sides exposed to you.

The forearm deflection is a good technique when properly applied. Even if you're kicked when you move in, it won't be with as much power as if you had stayed just outside your safe distance and in his most effective kicking range. So you must keep an opponent exactly within your safe distance—no closer, no farther. In this way you can efficiently deal with the initial movement of the kick instead of having to deal with the full brunt of a delivered kick.

Another technique you may use against a snap kick (or any other kick) is to kick his standing leg as he starts to kick you (Fig. 53). This is especially effective because it makes you the attacker at his invitation. When his kick is checked at the start, it will generally throw his balance off sufficiently for you to counter with whatever method you want without too much risk of his recovering in time to kick you again.

Something to keep in mind when watching for telegraphic movement in kicks is that the upper thigh will move well ahead of the following kick. Generally, but not always, the torso will lean back as the kick is initiated, and there may be a brief shuffle of feet before he kicks.

The second kick you're most likely to encounter is a roundhouse. This kick is usually preceded by an abrupt lifting of the upper thigh and knee and then the delivery. This telegraphic movement is normally easier to detect than the ones associated with the snap kick.

As your partner launches his kick, drop to your right knee to duck under the kick, and then punch up into the groin Even if he kicks low at the last minute, your body position (on your knee, with left hand up to protect) should give

Figure 53

Figure 54

you sufficient protection to still punch up into the groin. He will be completely exposed. These, of course, are defenses against kicks launched outside your safe distance in which you must now deal with the fully delivered kick(Fig. 54).

There are several variations of this technique. One is to drop into a low crouch and duck under his kick, then move up behind him to attack his back or grab his hair and take him down to the ground. You can also crouch down and roundhouse-kick his standing leg as in a sweep to take him down. Another variation would be to step into him and capture his kicking leg, and then kick his standing leg out from under him (Fig. 55).

When you execute these techniques, be alert to your opponent's hands; you haven't hurt him or taken him down when you capture the leg, and in the time it takes you to kick his leg out from under him, he can still punch you. This being the case, you should get your entry and technique down to the point where you can kick his standing leg out from under him in the same instant that you capture his kicking leg.

Do this technique (as well as the others) until you are proficient against whichever leg the opponent kicks with. Try not to anticipate his kick or what technique you're going to employ. Herein lies the principal advantage of knowing more than one technique; if you thought your partner was going to deliver a right kick and you set yourself to do the technique as shown in Fig. 55, and he instead delivers a left kick, it's a simple matter to drop to a crouch and utilize a technique such as that shown in Fig. 54.

I realize all that advice sounds complicated when you consider that the kick takes place in an instant; but my point is that if you move at the initial telegraphic movement without hesitation, you'll be able to execute a variation of any or all kicking defenses spontaneously if you have practiced diligently. It is you who will reap the benefits of the training and practice and your skill will be commensurate with your effort.

Another method of dealing with a roundhouse kick would be to snap-kick him in the groin as he lifts his leg in a round-

Figure 55

Figure 56

house motion (Fig. 56). This is similar to one of the earlier techniques in this chapter, except instead of kicking his leg to stop him, you kick to a vulnerable area that he exposes to you when delivering a roundhouse kick.

In addition to the techniques I'm putting forth here, don't exclude using windmill-type deflections or outgrabs as a viable method of kick defense. As you and your partner begin practicing these techniques, you should soon discover what feels most comfortable for you so you are aware of the techniques and variations you can have the most confidence in.

The next kick defense for you to practice will be against spinning kicks. These kicks are generally easier to detect than the previous kicks we covered, but know this: if you remain where you are or back-pedal slightly, you will be hit almost every time.

To begin practicing against these kicks, study the accompanying figures beforehand. Having done that, have your partner throw a spinning kick or as close an imitation as he can manage (refer back to the mechanics of this kick earlier in this chapter).

Drop to a low crouch as you see him turn his hips and begin his kick. You can then roundhouse-kick or sweep his standing leg out from under him (Fig. 57). When you crouch, do so with a step in to him so that you don't have to stretch out your leg just to reach his standing leg.

Another technique would be for you to step deep into him as he pivots so that you'll be directly behind him by the time his kick is launched. You can then capture his leg while it has expended its energy past you and then kick his standing leg out from under him (Fig. 58). Try these techniques against a hooking kick, too.

The next technique for you to try is simple and very similar to earlier defenses. As your opponent/partner begins his spin to kick you, simply kick his buttocks to abort the movement or the back of the knee to break him down. It's important that you do this at the start of the kick instead of when the leg straightens toward you. In this position he will be most

Figure 57

Figure 58

Figure 59

vulnerable, and you'll have a better chance to kick where you want without being knocked off balance (Fig. 59).

Yet another technique for dealing with a spinning kick would be for you to again duck under his kicking leg until it has passed over you, and then raise up in front of him to clutch his throat and groin to either take him down or injure him (Fig. 60). You also have the option of letting his kick pass overhead and returning with a kick of your own to his vital areas.

Figure 60

Remember that these kicks can be very quick and power-ful when delivered by the right person—therefore you must assume that whoever your opponent is has this ability to injure you, and then be as cautious and alert as you can without losing confidence in your own abilities.

Another kick that's popular with martial artists is a fly-ing kick. In almost any kung fu or karate movie, one often sees the hero and villain alike leaping through the air to deliver kicks at each other. And while this is all very dramatic, it's seldom necessary or as effective as the movies would have you believe.

The principal advantage to a flying kick lies in the momen-tum, weight of the body, and speed when hitting an inert object. If all these conditions are met, it can be a powerful kick indeed. The disadvantage to this type of kick is that once the kicker leaves the ground, he'll have no way to recover balance and control if his kick is disrupted, he misses, or his kick is deflected.

Before you and your partner practice defenses against flying kicks, you must find a soft surface to work on, such as a mattress, mat, or pads. Since you will each be falling quite a bit as a result of these techniques, try not to break your fall with your arms straight down; you could hurt your wrists or arms in this way. Instead, splay your arms to the sides and slap the surface as you land to absorb the shock (refer to Chapter 5 on how to fall).

To defend against a flying kick, have your partner take a leap and kick at you, using a side kick, for instance. As his kick comes to you, side-step and pull your arm up under his kicking leg (Fig. 61). When you do this, you deprive him of time to recover from your pulling maneuver, and he does not have time to plan a countermove.

After you do this technique and feel comfortable with it, you should kick your partner in the same manner so that you will feel the helpless sensation in having been thwarted and falling to the ground.

The next technique for you to try, once your partner kicks at you again, would be for you to crouch under his kick and

Figure 61

Figure 62

raise up sharply to topple him (Fig. 62). In this way you'll be able to capture one or both of his legs and have control over him as he lands.

If you have established your safe distance and are watchful for telegraphic movements, you should have little problem in dealing with flying or jump kicks. Even if your timing is off and your execution of technique fails, you will at least have had an opportunity to shift your body so that it will be a glancing blow instead of receiving the full impact.

You must practice these techniques until they become second nature to you. Practice so your movements harmonize with those of your opponent. Practice so you'll possess the confidence to employ them at the time you need them, doing so without hesitation. And finally, by developing your own kicking skills, you can be more aware of an opponent's subtle and overt movements, weight shifts, and intent.

Chapter 3

━━━━━━

LI GA: HARMONY OF BALANCE IN MOVEMENT

The Li Ga family concerns itself primarily with the power in movement that we all have, if we only knew it. The power is essentially rooted in the feet, develops in the legs, is directed by the waist, and functions through the fingers. The energy potential in any given movement, whether peaceful and benign or intense and violent, can be likened most to the eye of a hurricane. A hurricane is at once calm at its epicenter and violent to the extreme at its periphery.

Li Ga can best be learned and appreciated through the application of leverage principles. While the leverage techniques in and of themselves are immediately street-applicable, consider the techniques throughout this chapter to be a vehicle to understand and apply Li Ga to discover a force within you that is at once simple and subtle—and yet so very much more!

I'll begin this topic by pointing out that escape from grips and holds will be practically unnecessary if you simply become alert to an impending attack and don't pretend it isn't happening! If you're aware of an intent to grab or hold you, then you should attack your opponent before the hold is accomplished. If you delay your escape too long, even a second, then you may become too disoriented or hampered to effectively deal with it.

During the practical applications of these techniques, I would like to stress the importance of a partner not releasing a hold until you actually escape. The reason for this is simple; if you're the one applying the hold and you release your partner even though he didn't actually escape, you'll have done more harm than good. If your partner believes himself capable of a technique and attempts to apply it in a real situation, he could provoke the assailant to do more harm than he might have planned. So, with this in mind, let's begin to do something about it.

Wrist Grabs

To start, we'll look into a pretty common type of assault—wrist grabs. Numerous attacks on women have been preceded by the attacker grabbing the arm or wrist and pulling the victim into a car or bushes. Men have also been grabbed and pulled into alleys to be robbed or beaten.

So to begin, grab your partner's wrist and pull him across the room while he struggles to get free. Then have your partner grab you and see if you can free yourself.

If you were unable to free yourself, there's a very good reason why; you probably tried to pull back or against your partner's other fingers. Instead, after your wrist has been grabbed, pull up against the thumb—sharply! This way you're only pulling against his thumb, instead of all his fingers. When your partner grabs your wrist with both hands, again pull sharply against and away from his thumbs (Fig. 63).

If you are unable to accomplish this because of his superior strength, then simply grab the front of your own hand and step back as you lift your hand out of his grasp, *sharply!* In this fashion, your body weight will assist the sharp pull against his thumbs (Fig. 64).

Another method would be to reach over his hands and grab your own, and then twist your hand up and over his hands (Fig. 65). This can be accomplished in either direc-

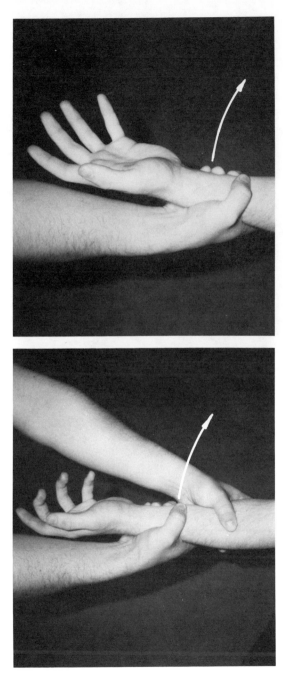

Figure 63

Figure 64

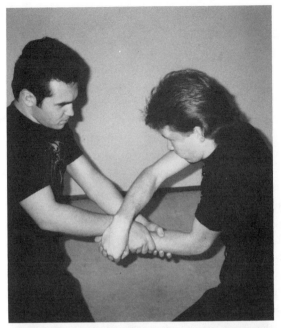

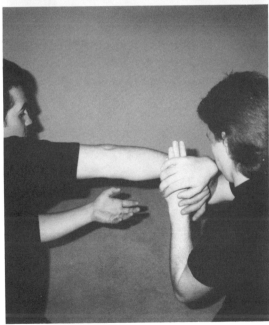

Figure 65

tion. It will also be to your advantage to step in the same direction as you rotate your hand. In this way you'll have leverage and your body weight to assist you, and it will leave him exposed to your own attack.

If an attacker jerks you off balance (have your partner do it), simply follow along and jam him. Press your free hand atop his and then step between his legs, pushing his hands to the ground. This should put him off balance and cause him to fall on his butt (Fig. 66).

In each of the above instances of dealing with escapes from wrist grabs, you will have applied a logical leverage/physics principle, in that you utilized a superior force to a seemingly hopeless situation. You see, when you have knowledge of how to use your body, you can act calmly in the face of a violent encounter.

Now that you're beginning to understand that there's more to fighting than flailing arms and legs, let's look at another aspect of the application of Li Ga principles of leverage and body movement.

Choke Holds

Considering the simplicity of the techniques involved in escaping a frontal choke hold, it still surprises me when I read of someone being strangled. The escapes are extremely simple and effective.

Seldom, if ever, will an opponent have his arms fully extended while choking someone. I've seen instructors and books try to teach defense from a choke hold in this manner, and it's a damn shame. Almost always there is a violent shaking of the victim to disorient as well as to cut off the oxygen supply.

For training purposes, you and your partner may refrain from using full force, since it's difficult to read instructions with your eyes bulging and tongue hanging out from a strangle hold. Once you feel sufficiently confident with the techniques, then by all means use more force on each other.

To begin, have your partner choke you. As he does so, step in and to his left with your left foot as you jab into his windpipe with your right index finger (Fig. 67).

Figure 66

Figure 67

When you stepped in to him you increased your reach with the step, and by turning your torso to jab his windpipe, you cut off his oxygen supply with your right index finger jab. If your partner has considerably longer reach than you even after you've stepped in, then you should immediately flow into another technique. The following is a very good alternative.

As your partner chokes you, swing your right arm up and over to your left as you turn your torso to the left (Fig. 68). It's important that you bring your right arm straight up in order to achieve the proper leverage. If you lower your arm so it's more horizontal, you'll only succeed in forcing his hand nearest your right arm to tighten around your neck. So again, you will want to bring your arm up and over as near to vertical as you possibly can. Practice and see the difference; this is a great technique!

After you practice and accomplish this technique, do it again, only this time pivot a complete 360 degrees to your left, and the opponent's entire left side will be open and exposed to you. Take advantage! The beauty of this technique is the ability to incorporate your center in a pivot,

Figure 68

using minimal effort and energy, without relying on the strength of your limbs.

The next technique against a frontal choke involves a bit more leverage. As your partner chokes you, clasp one of your hands atop the other below his arm so that you form a wedge with your forearms. Now shoot both your arms straight up between his arms at the wrists.

If you do this with your arms partially extended, you'll be pitting your strength against his. However, if you launch your hands straight up and against the wrists, you'll gain the proper leverage with which to free yourself. You can also step back as you do this technique to utilize your body weight; after you've broken free, you'll be in a good position to step forward and hammer down to his nose with your wrist (Fig. 69).

Another type of leverage escape from a choke hold would be to lay your right forearm over his left forearm and then under his right forearm. Grab your right hand with your left to lift it up and over to the right, using your arms in much the same way as a lever and fulcrum (Fig. 70). At this point, both of your opponent's hands will be at your right

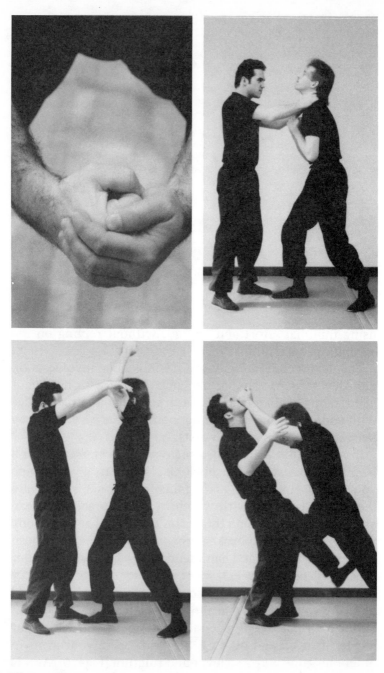

Figure 69

side, thus leaving him in an extremely vulnerable position; *take advantage!*

There are other techniques and escapes from these various holds and situations, but we'll just work on a few of them. You'll more likely retain a technique at this point if you learn a few, make variations, and work them well rather than being familiar with dozens that you aren't too sure about. You're primarily acquiring movement skills instead of memorizing techniques; as a rule of thumb, if you're straining and using strength, you're probably doing it poorly.

There are a few more simple things you can do when you're first grabbed in a frontal choke hold. You can kick or knee into the groin, knee, or shin; pinch hard to the sensitive underside of the biceps, or do anything else you can think of at the moment to cause sudden pain and injury. *Be aware!* Don't wait until your eyes begin to bulge and water before you begin to free yourself. React the very instant he touches you or you think he's going to touch you.

On a choke hold from behind, the first thing *not* to do is struggle uselessly and flop around like a carp out of water. I realize that sounds like unnecessary advice, but it can literally mean the difference between life and death.

If you are being choked from behind, you can place your hands atop those of your assailant's and pivot around (either direction) into him and kick him (do it a few times right now), or you can grip his hands and twist your body all the way around to loosen or get free of his grip (Fig. 71). You can also kick backward into the legs or groin.

You can grab his left hand with your left hand and twist it counterclockwise to release his grip (or your right hand to his right hand and twist clockwise). These techniques should be done with a high degree of suddenness. If you falter, you'll give the opponent time to counter anything you try in the way of escaping.

If someone is choking you from behind with his forearm, the first thing for you to do is turn your head in the direction of his elbow. Your throat won't be so constricted in the crook of his elbow, and if you're able, bite into his arm as hard as you can.

Figure 70

Practice each of these escapes as I've described them, and then try this one. Have your partner choke you from behind with his right forearm, and hold onto it with both hands. Then bring your left leg behind his right leg; turn to your left into him to trip him over your left leg. I know it all sounds confusing; just read this again slowly, see Figure 72, and go through it with your partner. Do it now and then try it with his other arm.

Another alternative would be to stomp to the top of his foot or along his shin, and elbow-strike to the ribs. For the sake of learning and practice, examine your position and situation and think of something to do yourself. You *can* do it. Problem solving is a practical aspect of any endeavor you will get involved in, and fighting is no exception.

Headlocks

Let's now move on to headlocks. You may find yourself wrapped in a headlock in many given instances, none of which are excusable. Does that disturb you? It shouldn't; if you had properly applied the principles and concepts I've

Figure 71

Figure 72

shared with you up to this point, you will have dealt with your opponent before he put you in a grappling position, enabling him to effect a headlock or any other hold on you.

However, the single common denominator we all share, regardless of rank and ability, is that we're human and therefore subject to errors in judgment, timing, and execution of technique. It's under this premise that you should pay all the more attention to what you're doing, and practice diligently.

Now let's do something about those headlocks. If you're struggling with someone and find yourself placed in a headlock, don't panic and thrash about. Act at once before you become disoriented. If it's a family member or a friend indulging in a little horseplay, you can bring sufficient pain to bear without actually injuring him. If it's a stranger, you should be prepared to hurt him.

Have your partner place you in a headlock with his right arm (afterward do it with the left). As you're put in the hold, reach your left arm up and over his head so that your left hand comes down over his face, and then press your index finger horizontally under his nose and press upward, pressing the cartilage inward and upward (Fig. 73). You should find that this can be *very* painful.

Another technique would be to pinch the tender area of his inner thigh with your left hand (which will be the hand closest to his leg without your actually having to reach around him). When you pinch, try to get a small amount of skin between the thumb and index finger, then pinch and twist the skin to create the most pain (Fig. 74).

You can also punch up into the groin with the right hand. Punch repeatedly if you must and punch hard! He won't be able to take very much of that (Fig. 75).

Yet another method would be to lift your leg and launch it back between his legs as you strike him to the back of the head with your left forearm. You would do these two things at the same time for maximum effect (Fig. 76).

Before we continue any further, I want you to note that each of the techniques you've done so far has been accomplished with little actual effort. And as you do them

Figure 73

Figure 74

Figure 75

Figure 76

again, pay special attention to the fact that the closer to your center of gravity and body line, the more power you have. If you have to reach for him to hit, pinch, or strike in any manner, then get closer to him to occupy his center of gravity and you'll see the additional force you can add to whatever strike you make.

Arm Pins

One of the more common holds people use to force someone to go where they want them to is to pin their opponent's arm behind them. If someone has your arm pinned behind your back, you aren't as helpless as you might imagine. Depending on the variations of this hold, there are several things you can do. Let's examine a few possibilities right now.

Have your partner pin your left arm behind your back, and then take a moment to assess your situation; determine what you can and can't do. The hold itself dictates that you raise up on your toes to ease the pain. You can alleviate the pain as you apply an escape technique. For instance, as your partner pins your left arm behind you, step forward and to the left with your right foot as you pivot to your left under your left arm (Fig. 77). This motion will take the pressure off your shoulder and put you in a good position to counterattack.

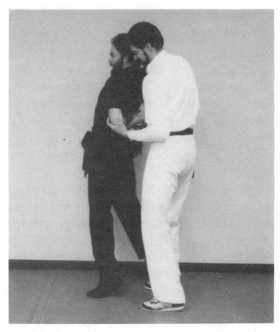

Figure 77

Another method would be to step to the left with your left foot as you strike to the groin with your right hand (Fig. 78). Or step back between his legs with your right leg, delivering a right elbow strike to the solar plexus, throat, face, or whichever target is most accessible to you (Fig. 79).

The latter technique would be especially effective if an opponent were to pull you in any direction under this hold. The first technique we covered for an arm pin would be a good escape if the opponent were to push you in any direction.

As you can see, you still have tools available to you even with your arm pinned behind you. At the expense of becoming repititious, however, I'm going to stress to you again: *don't allow yourself to get caught in a hold!* That statement is so simple, it's easy to underestimate its significance. When you and your partner begin working out or are simply practicing escapes, note the instant you realize or feel a hold is coming and how long it takes you to react to it. Ideally, you'll respond as your opponent reaches for you or as soon as you feel his touch.

Figure 78

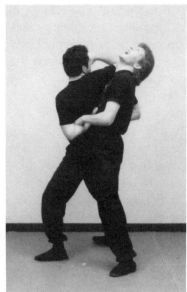

Figure 79

It'll be a good training exercise for you both to really try to establish a hold during the course of a workout. In this way you can acquire the habit of fending off or attacking at the first indication of an attempt to put you into a hold of any kind.

Moreover, when you and your partner practice escapes, make variations of the hold, analyze the situation, and see the possibilities open to you. Ask your partner for suggestions; after all, he's the one who has you in the hold, and he can see things from a different angle. Then you do the same.

Handshakes

There are occasions when we meet new people or greet old acquaintances who feel compelled to crush our hand during a handshake. Invariably they'll have a laugh at our expense, as well as entertaining anyone else who happens to be present.

It's important that you not let them get away with this

for many reasons. First of all, if you let him get away with it, he might feel compelled to progress into some jostling, shoving, or general horseplay to further enhance his power over you and the imagined adulation of his many presumed admirers.

Every day, in every way, you teach people how you'll be treated. In word, action, and deed, you convey to everyone how you *will* be treated, not necessarily how you *want* to be. Think about this for a moment. If someone grips your hand in a crushing grip and you do nothing but smile weakly, you've taught him you'll accept physical humiliation. Encouraged by this, you can just bet that relations with your newfound friend will go steadily downhill.

Secondly, when you begin from a position of strength (yet maintaining an easy manner), you'll maintain your own confidence, and diminish his! In time you'll come to see the importance and significance in this, if you don't already.

To begin, I'll illustrate a few techniques to make the other guy dance in pain as he would have you do. But before we start, a little discretion is advised. There are those who are truly unaware of the discomfort you're feeling, and to their knowledge they're simply giving a strong, masculine hand-shake (the old-fashioned palm-to-palm). You'll know who they are, and you should give a firm handshake in return—in fact, you should always give a firm handshake. Whether you know it or not, a great many men are insulted by a limp handshake.

Now, have your partner give you a firm grip. As he begins to squeeze you, lift your thumb and hook your left index finger down and under your thumb (Fig. 80). Now drive the second knuckle of your left index finger into the bone of his right hand that runs from the juncture of his thumb to the index finger. You can bring more pressure to bear by using your right thumb to squeeze your finger into his hand. If this technique is executed properly and with enough pressure, it should cause the other man to buckle at the knees and go to the ground.

Another method is to relax your grip so you can grab his little finger, and then roll your hand so his palm is up and

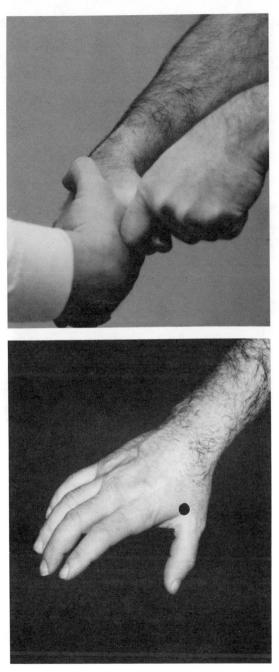

Figure 80

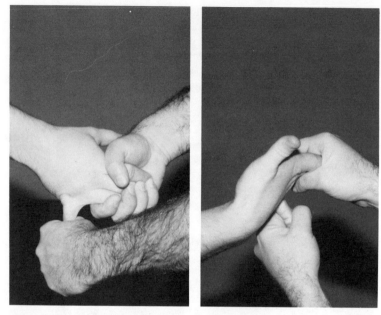

Figure 81

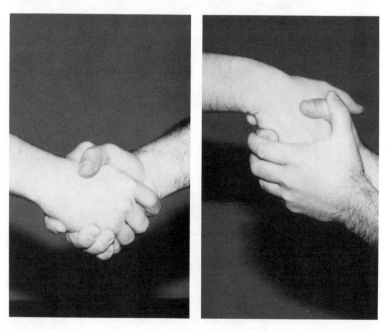

Figure 82

crank back on his little finger. This should loosen his grip enough for you to slide your hand slightly back so that you can grip the top of his other fingers; then lift up on his finger tips as you pull back on his little finger (Fig. 81).

This technique should serve to lift the other man on his tiptoes to try to get away from the pain in his hand. When you do this, remember that his palm should face upward and his little finger should move back in to him. This is an effective and painful technique; you'll have it within your power to break his fingers if the situation should warrant it.

Another technique would be to bring your left hand up under your right, and then lift up on his hand with both of yours. When you do this, bring your hands up and in to you; this will put a great deal of pressure on his wrists when you do this because of the leverage you'll have (Fig. 82).

A word of caution here. Do these techniques with your partner slowly and steadily to find the results you want. If you do this fast at the start, you could injure your partner. This note of caution applies to all the techniques in this book.

Grabs

Another common hold you're likely to encounter occurs when you're confronted by someone who grabs your shirt front in his fist and threatens you with bodily harm. There are several ways of dealing with this type of assault, and we'll examine a few right now.

First of all, take the responsibility to initiate sudden violence! The only way he could grab your shirt front is if you let him. The very instant he invaded your safe distance with his reach to your shirt front should trigger your attack response! When a situation becomes tense, become a predator!

Start by having your partner grab your shirt front with his right hand (left later) (presuming you are distracted by something or someone and you find yourself in this grip). To see the full impact of this simple and effective technique, tell your partner to hold on as tight as he can and to do his best not to let go of you. Now reach up under and slightly

Figure 83

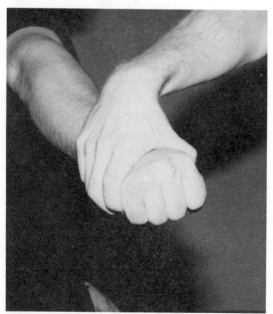

Figure 84

behind the biceps, a very tender area, and pinch hard and sudden! He *will* let you go (Fig. 83). Practice this technique using your arm nearest his grabbing arm so he won't be as apt to notice what you're doing.

Another method is to apply a wrist leverage. This is accomplished by grabbing the top of his hand with your right thumb pressed between his thumb and index finger and the rest of your fingers pressed to the side of his hand (Fig. 84). Once you grab his hand in this manner, twist it so that your thumb pushes the juncture of his thumb and finger while your other fingers pull. Twist his hand to the right and push down with the torque on his wrist and you should be able to take him to the ground.

When a man grabs you in such a fashion, he certainly means you no good; depending upon the situation, a swift kick in the shin is as good a deterrent as any.

Another aspect of grabs worth delving into is if two men should grab you. If they clutch your arms and pull in opposite directions, for possibly a third to work you over or rob you, you have a few options at your disposal. First of all, when they're pulling your arms apart, one of them will invariably pull harder than the other. If you try to kick either one of them, you probably wouldn't be able to do so with any telling effect (Fig. 85a).

However, if you take a sideward step in the direction of the man who is pulling hardest, it will then be you and he pulling the other man (Fig. 85b) well within kicking range (Fig. 85c). Kick him, repeatedly if necessary, and then deal with the other man.

If you're being held under the arms and led along, you can sweep-kick the foot of either man out from under him and stomp to the back of his other knee to bring him down. You can then attack with the severity the situation warrants.

Another option would be to stomp the ankle nearest you to either take the man down or to loosen his grip enough for you to escape his hold and deal with the other man.

It still comes back to being aware of their presence in the

Figure 85a

Figure 85b

Figure 85c

first place and remaining vigilant if you suspect you may be attacked. If you must walk on a sidewalk late at night or even in daylight, good neighborhood or bad, walk in the middle and be watchful around parked cars, alleys, fences, hedges, or any place that might offer concealment. Be alert to footsteps approaching from behind or from the front, and to people loitering in doorways.

Position yourself in such a way that you can utilize your peripheral vision to detect movement from any place in the immediate area. If you are on a sidewalk downtown, utilize the reflection of storefront windows to see behind you as you walk. You don't have to be paranoid, simply be aware.

Hair Techniques

Another common grab you're likely to encounter is a hair grab. If an occasion should arise where someone grabs you by the hair and jerks you about, you'll find that it's difficult to think and act because of the degree of pain involved. Knowing this, you will naturally want to get out of such a grab as soon as you can.

So, to begin, have your partner grab you by the hair with his right hand. Place your right hand on top of his, as shown earlier in Figure 84. Lean your head down and to the right as you lock out his elbow with your left hand.

As you lean down to release his hand from your hair, he should end up in a position where his right palm is up in your grasp and his body bent over. His arm should be locked out as you should now have him in a hold to do with as you please (Fig. 86).

Now that you've gotten out of a hair grab, let's get on to putting someone else into a hair control situation to teach your attacker what pain is all about.

When most people grab hair, they often just grab a handful and start pulling. To do this correctly, slide your hand through the hair along the scalp, and then clutch the hair in your fist. In this fashion you not only generate a lot more pain by having hold of more nerve endings, but you'll also have a higher degree of control over an opponent (Fig. 87).

Figure 86

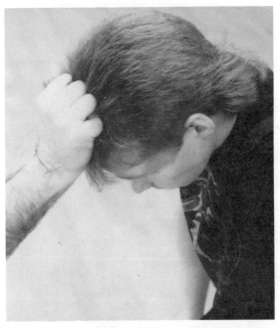

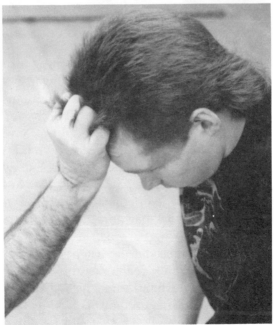

Figure 87

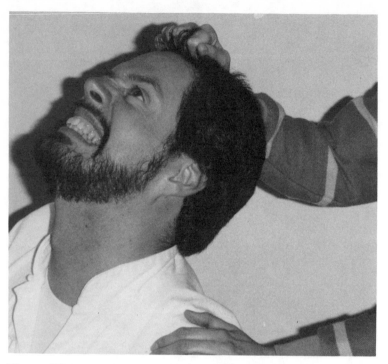

Figure 88a

The hair can be a crucial aid in controlling a person. If you wish to take an opponent down backwards, grab the hair at the hairline on the forehead and then snap it backward and down (Fig. 88a). This will be better learned and remembered if you go through it right now with your partner. It's important to snap the head down on this technique, because if you simply pulled the hair backward, the opponent could stumble away from you. By yanking the head down, you'll pile the opponent at your feet (do these techniques slowly on your partner, but do it fast and hard on an attacker).

To turn an opponent so that he has his back exposed to you from a frontal assault, reach past his head with your right hand and clutch the hair nearest his right ear (Fig. 88b); now yank his head around so that his back is to you, and do with him what you will. This should be done quickly enough to turn his body without breaking his neck.

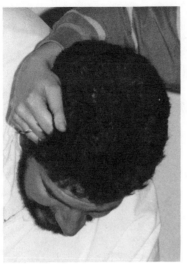 

Figure 88b

Another method of hair control is to direct the head forward and down. This can be accomplished by grabbing the hair at the back of the head and then yanking forward and down, putting your shoulder into it for leverage (Fig. 88c).

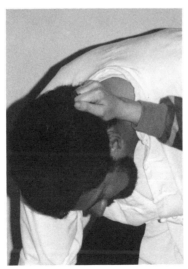 

Figure 88c

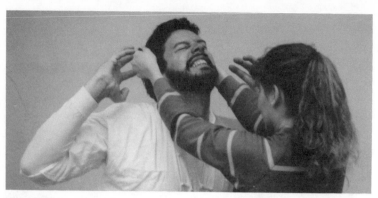

Figure 89a

Yet another method of control would be to grab the hair at both sides of the head (Fig. 89a) and twist his head backward and down. You can do this with just your wrists if you are of the same height as your opponent; if he's taller than you, you must bring his head down to you by utilizing the pain principle (stomp his foot, knee, shin, or groin) and stepping over his lead leg with one of yours to force him down at your feet (Fig. 89b).

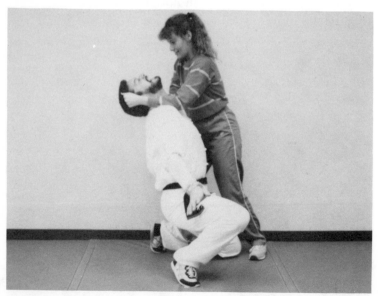

Figure 89b

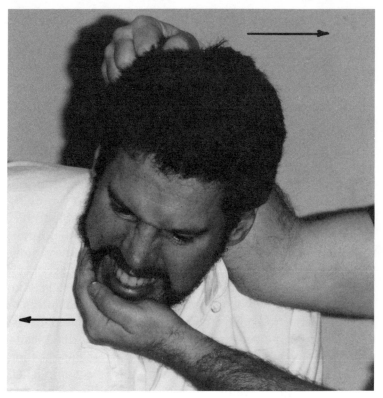

Figure 90

Hair techniques are excellent control methods against people you must defend yourself from but don't want to injure. If on the other hand your life is in danger, you can break a man's neck by employing a hair technique. To do this, grab the hair at the back of the head with one hand and cup the chin with the other. Once you have the head in this position, pull the hair and push the chin sharply! (Fig. 90)

When you practice this with your partner *be careful!* If the technique is applied too strongly, you can cause severe permanent damage. This technique can be applied in a second and it can cripple or kill in a heartbeat!

By now there is bound to be someone reading this who is wondering what to do if the opponent has no hair or if he has a wig. If you attempt these or any other techniques and they don't come off as you thought they would, then keep right on attacking; don't stop just because something went wrong. As to the dilemma of what to do if the opponent is bald and you want to control him, you can use his ears or eye sockets as substitutes. Experiment and see which is easiest for you.

Takedowns

Through the Li Ga principles and techniques of san soo, you should begin to realize the power you have simply by utilizing your body efficiently. You should be able to feel when you're operating from a balanced (centered) position and the resultant force you have at your command simply by letting your body do the work you had previously been doing with just your limbs. Through the rest of the text, take further notice how you can achieve significant advances in the application of balanced power in your movement skills.

A particularly useful way to employ Li Ga principles of balance, movement, and leverage is through the application of takedown techniques. Takedowns can be accomplished without a lot of grappling, slugging, and scuffling. They can be a quick and efficient means of ending a violent attack without it deteriorating into a bloody slugfest—for both of you.

For simplification, most of the techniques will be initiated with a right punch. Once you have the technique worked out to your satisfaction, it'll be up to you and your partner to apply the techniques to left punches, low punches, jabs, hooks, combinations, etc.

We'll start with an easy takedown. Have your partner deliver you a right punch. Step past and to the left of him and stomp to the back of his knee on the leg nearest you. This action will force him down at your feet (Fig. 91). Now stand on his leg where you stomped and grind his kneecap into the ground (don't do this to your partner). Give the back of his knee a pretty good shot or you'll only buckle him instead of taking him down. If it should happen that you

Figure 91

only buckle his leg, you can follow up immediately by stomping on the back of the other knee. You can also stomp to the inside or outside of the ankle to take him down.

The next takedown is fast and effective and is similar to the last one. As your partner delivers a right punch, step past and to the left of him as you guide the punch past. Reach up under his right arm (or over it if he brings his arm back) and grab his throat with your hand as you launch your right leg back underneath his right leg to take him down (Fig. 92).

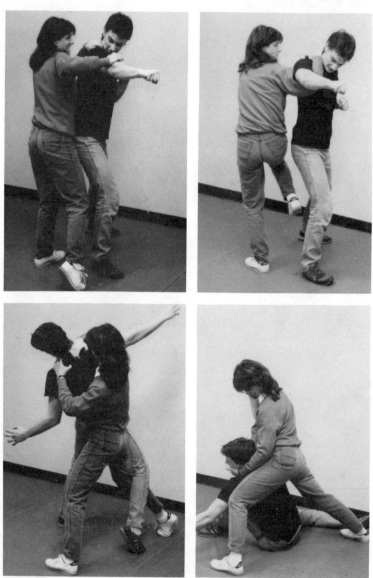

Figure 92

When you do this, extend your leg and place your foot down well ahead of his. In this way you'll achieve the proper reach and lift to take him down (keep your head up and in line with your groin). You should make fast and hard impact

Figure 93

to the back of his knee with the back of yours to get the necessary impact and power to achieve a quick takedown.

The next takedown begins the same as the others; this time bring your right arm up under his right arm and around his neck, hold him tightly as you knee him in the solar plexus or groin, and then drop to your right knee to take him down with you (Fig. 93). If you want to make a quicker takedown, eliminate the knee to the solar plexus.

You can deflect or guide the punch past as you step deep into the middle of him, with your leading leg between and in past his as you palm punch-push down to the inside hip of his leading leg. Try to palm down as your foot sets down (Fig. 94a).

After you've made your entry, grip your partner's head in the manner of a neck snap (right hand in his hair at the back of his head, left hand cups the chin) and pull the hair and push the chin. Instead of snapping the neck as before, simply twist to the right as you drop to your right knee (Fig. 94b). Do this slowly on your partner.

For the last takedown, after your partner punches, step with your right foot between and just behind his leading

Figure 94a

Figure 94b

leg (in this case his right foot). Angle your right foot behind his heel so he can't back up, then press your shin into his. You can lean into his leg to take him down or even go down on your right knee if that's what it takes (Fig. 94c).

Figure 94c

Fighting From the Ground

After you've practiced these takedowns and made variations on them, it'll be time to practice takedowns from a kneeling position. You can use this type of takedown technique on its own or to follow up after a kick from the ground.

A takedown will put you in a superior position to deal with an opponent's attack because when it's carried off successfully, it will hurt, disorient, and put him in a defensive position to which he will most likely be unaccustomed. It'll be much easier to deal with him at your own level as well.

Your first takedown will be simple. Have your partner stand before you as though trying to intimidate and harass you. From your kneeling position, lunge and punch with both hands to the groin (Fig. 95). Since it is your partner and not an actual attacker, simply push with both hands to the hips (I just know your partner will appreciate the difference).

With this technique, be sure your partner is close enough to you to get the right amount of force necessary to fold him over. If he's too far away, you'll only serve to bend him at

Figure 95

the waist and leave yourself in an extremely vulnerable position. If you do this correctly, it should drop him on his butt directly in front of you. At that point you can twist his ankle to turn him over and make him more vulnerable and accessible to you while you get to your feet and finish him off.

The next technique involves a leg sweep. This will be accomplished in much the same way as a roundhouse kick—the only difference is that you'll kick past the opponent's leg. To better facilitate the sweep, you'll want to kick with your instep or lower shin to the bottom of the opponent's foot, anywhere in the area of the Achilles tendon. By sweeping his leg in this place, you'll gain better leverage to take him down (Fig. 96).

You may practice this a few times (I say a few times because practicing this particular technique can become very painful very shortly) until you can take him down every time you try. There is no way you can do this type of sweep gently with each other and still achieve the correct takedown.

The leg sweep can be used on an opponent who is standing in front of or approaching you. When you sweep an attacker

Figure 96

who's coming at you, it's best to sweep his nearest leg. This is an extremely effective takedown which will often knock the wind out of an attacker when he lands, or will just as often make him hit his head, elbow, wrist, or hip hard enough to disable him if he falls on a hard surface.

Another type of takedown from the ground is a body roll takedown. To do this, have your partner stand in front of you within easy reach. Now reach around his right leg with your right arm and grip him behind the ankle. This will anchor his leg to the ground so he won't escape while you wrap your upper arm behind his calf and roll into him (Fig. 97). This will lever him to the ground and onto his back.

Figure 97

This takedown should place you atop your partner's right leg, with your partner feeling a degree of stress on his leg at the knee. You will be in a good position to left-elbow strike to the groin. Try this technique off the opposite leg when you feel comfortable with it and you'll be able to take him down no matter which leg is nearest you. This is also a very effective technique to use even if you're already standing, whether an opponent punches or not. You can drop to a knee or a low crouch and take him down the same as before.

Another technique similar to the body roll is to grab behind the opponent's right foot with your left hand as you use your right forearm to press his right knee (Fig. 98). This action

Figure 98

will lever him to the ground. These techniques should be done as quickly as possible once you decide to do them, otherwise an opponent can escape.

In the case of an opponent standing before you with his feet spread evenly apart, you can drop him to the ground by shoving your right foot against the inside of his left ankle as you push to the inside of his right ankle with your right palm or forearm (Fig. 99).

This takedown has the added advantage that when the opponent falls, his legs will be widespread, leaving him vulnerable to a hard kick to his exposed and unprotected groin.

Figure 99

If an opponent punches at you while you're sitting or kneeling, you'll always have the option of outgrabbing, windmilling, or guiding his punch past you as we covered previously (Fig. 100). Once the punch is past you, the opponent will have his head near enough for you to execute a hair technique and put him under your control.

Figure 100

A situation that is not too common but happens often enough to mention is when someone is standing directly behind you while you're sitting on the ground. This is not only annoying, but potentially dangerous as well. If the person is within easy reach of you, you can reach behind and grab the back of his heels, then bow your back sharply against his knees to take him down (Fig. 101).

This will have a whip-like effect on his upper body and drop him without too much chance of real harm. If you do wish to injure him, it will be a simple matter to pivot around on one knee to put yourself in a position to better deal with him. When you practice this with your partner, each of you must be especially careful to protect yourselves when you fall (see how to fall in Chapter 5).

Remember, you're only as safe as you allow yourself to be! Unless you are caught totally unaware and unprepared, you should be able to successfully defend yourself to the extent you're willing to hurt someone!

Figure 101

If you should ever find yourself in a grappling situation and end up on the bottom, or are toppled and the attacker straddles your chest or is lying atop of you, there is something you can do about it. In this portion of learning and practicing Li Ga movement skills, we'll deal with the two most common types of positions with the opponent on top of you.

The first one is where the opponent sits astride your chest with his knees at your sides or pinning your arms; have your partner assume this position on you (Fig. 102a).

Figure 102a

Once your partner settles his weight on you, you must do two things at once—it's important that you do these simultaneously to achieve the proper release. You must jerk both your arms to your sides suddenly as you kick him sharply to the buttocks with either or both knees (Fig. 102b).

This action should launch your partner forward off your chest and onto his head on the floor above you. Your partner should be careful to protect himself on this takedown, since it's possible for him to hurt his head if it's a hard floor. Try to do this as well as the other techniques on a carpeted floor to minimize injury to yourself and your partner.

Another common position you may find yourself in is with the opponent lying atop your body lengthwise (I'll let you figure out how that could happen). See Fig. 103a. Have your partner lie atop you as described. Now simply reach your right hand over his head to grab the hair nearest his right

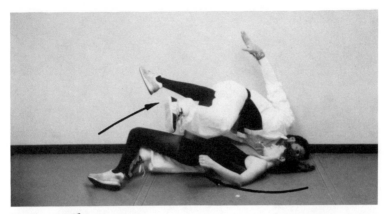

Figure 102b

Figure 103a

ear and yank sharply to the right, going easy on your partner (Fig. 103b). This will pull his body off the top of yours, and give you a chance to control him if you maintain your grip in his hair.

Other things you can do to an opponent on top of you are: kneeing him in the crotch if the opportunity is present; cupping your hands and clapping them together at his ears (for concussion); biting wherever you can reach; head-butt repeatedly to his face or temple, and wait for him to shift

Figure 103b

his position to strike you, hitting him with whatever limb becomes available.

There are a few things to keep in mind when you defend yourself from the ground. When an attacker punches or kicks at you, it's easier to guide past or deflect the blow than to intercept or exchange punches. There will usually be enough momentum behind the blow to bring his body, and thus his vital areas, within your reach.

As you and your partner practice these techniques, you should practice on different types of surfaces, and from different angles, practicing rolling out of the way to put yourself in a more strategic position to defend yourself or to attack your opponent.

If you have anything near at hand to use as a weapon, use it. A hard object will bring an attacker down to your level when whacked across his shins or knees. If at all possible, however, don't get caught on the ground. Though you now have some functional principles and techniques to apply, you can't afford a single handicap!

Multiple Attackers

If you are fortunate to have more than one partner studying with you, then you can practice defending against multiple attack. But before we get embroiled in this subject, I'd like you to consider a few things that may make you feel less intimidated should the occasion arise.

Imagine, if you will, that you and two others are going to beat up a man in the parking lot. Unless you and the others are a practiced team, it's likely that you will hit the man a few times and your cohorts will hit him a few times in a random, haphazard manner—effective to be sure, but hardly the work of trained professionals. So in a sense, you are each using little more than 30 percent of yourselves to beat up a man; this is against a man who, if he is actively going to defend himself, is using 100 percent of himself against each of you. So, theoretically, it would seem you are outnumbered. As military experts know, one man who knows what is going to happen is more effective than five who don't.

Taking this thought a step further, if you were surrounded by a dozen toughs and you stay within the circle, then you would definitely be up against the full dozen. However, if you were to suddenly flee and hit two of them simultaneously to effect your escape (attacking two is better than trying to run between them), the others will certainly follow. If they began to catch up with you and you gouge out the eyes of the first one to catch you, bite the nose off the next one, crush the throat of the next, and break the neck of the one after, it would be doubtful whether the rest would want to catch you.

I realize this is an extreme example, but it serves to illustrate my point about being the aggressor, being decisive, and utilizing maximum blood spillage to deter others from spilling yours! *You will do what you need to do to survive!*

I've often heard that when defending yourself from several men, it is best to get your back to the wall. I disagree; while it might be alright for some, it's more likely the attackers can stand in line until you fight yourself out. By taking flight you can better the odds, as I've already pointed out.

Sometimes place and circumstance can prevent you from immediate escape. This can be because you're in a closed room, crowded bar or party, or a one-way alley. In this case you can apply the following Li Ga movement skills.

The first is a movement to continue your opponent's momentum in another direction as you put him out of action, either temporarily or permanently. If you concentrate your attention too long on one attacker, another could finish you off; remember that!

Begin this exercise by having your partner deliver you a right punch. When he punches, step in and to the right of him with your right foot as you outgrab his punch with your left hand, clutching his left shoulder with your right hand. Then pivot on your right foot as you sweep your left leg around and behind you counterclockwise. Always maintain a hold on his arm and shoulder to neutralize further punches so that you can direct him 180 degrees from where he was. Study the photograph and go through the movement smoothly so that you don't interrupt his motion, but rather redirect him (Fig. 104).

Once you feel comfortable doing this, try to clutch his throat instead of his shoulder. In this way you have the option of crushing the windpipe or squeezing just hard enough to have control of him. When you've spun the man around, you can gouge the eyes, chop the neck or throat, kick the groin, etc., enabling you to deal with the next attacker quickly. You can even direct the first attacker into the second in this way, which will buy you time to deal with a third.

Another way you can incorporate this movement is to direct an attacker into a chair, wall, fire hydrant, or other solid object. In this way, the injury incurred by crashing into the object will have done your job well enough for you to deal with another attacker (Fig. 105).

Another option you would have in either a one-on-one or multiple attack situation would be to drop to one or both knees to punch out the groin when the attacker makes an initial movement (Fig. 106). You can also drop to one knee and kick up into him and then roll back up onto your feet.

Figure 104

The advantage of this type of movement is in its element of surprise as well as the position it puts you in to mete out punishment, with little immediate threat from the attacker.

If two or three men attack you at the same time, you can strike in two or three directions at the same time as well. If you're being approached from your left and your right, you can kick in one direction and punch in the other (Fig. 107).

Other alternatives include crouching and punching in opposite directions or punching to one side and kicking to

Figure 105

Figure 106

Figure 107

the other as you punch to the front with your other hand. You can direct one of them into another as we covered, and strike in different directions with whatever limbs are nearest to the attacker. Spend more time on this facet of defense than you think you ought to; vary the attacks and the angles so that the defender is busy. Now practice, experiment, and make variations to suit several situations of your own choosing.

After having practiced and mastered the principles and techniques of the Li Ga family, you can begin to internalize the harmony of balance in movement. The power and force I mentioned at the start of this chapter may have seemed to have something of the mystical quality that is often synonymous with the martial arts.

If this is the case with you, then I'll let you in on a big secret...You've had these qualities within you since you were born! Does that confuse you? In a very real sense, you aren't so different from the tin man, the lion, and the scarecrow from the *Wizard of Oz*. You, like they, have undergone and will yet undergo hardships and adventures to seek what you already have!

You have courage, you have heart, and you have brains. So what's the problem? The problem is that you (we) want more! That's the human condition; we all have what we need, and yet we want more, because only then can we truly be happy.

I opened this can of worms to drive home a point I've made throughout this book: if you want to get the most out of it, put the most into it! You already have the seeds of greatness within you, if you could only *believe it*. You already have the power of giants within you, if you could only *feel it*. You already have the courage and the conviction of a hero, if you would only *do it*.

Believe it; feel it; do it!

Chapter 4

FUT GA:
THE ESSENCE OF
SUDDEN VIOLENCE

Beginning students block an assault; experienced kung fu men attack after blocking; a Master has no need to block.

Anonymous

The Fut Ga family of kung fu san soo deals as much with the psychology of fighting as it does with the physical aspects. Fut Ga principles and techniques are entirely offense oriented, and so they rely on the intestinal fortitude (guts) of the practitioner to apply them with conviction and without hesitation. But above all else, Fut Ga is attitude. With Fut Ga, you become a predator.

You might ask just what this attitude has to do with self-defense, and how the psychology of men and fighting is related to a sudden violent situation. To get a firm grasp of this, we'll take a typical situation that may or may not precede a violent attack (but usually does).

Let's imagine you're at a bar or a party where someone else, typically a pseudo tough guy, tries to stare you down. This is merely a ruse to intimidate you, and if it succeeds, you can bet you're going to get better acquainted whether or not you want to.

You first notice this icy stare when you look in his general direction. He'll be bigger than you (and, of course, ugly goes without saying), and initially you may experience a sense of unease as you try to decide what to do or not do about him.

Before I tell you outright what to do, let's explore a couple of possibilities. First of all, as was touched on in the Li Ga chapter, you will teach him by word, action, and deed just what he thinks he can get away with. If you ignore him completely, you might be left alone. If you keep casting furtive glances at him to see if he's still watching you, he'll be encouraged by this, and you can figure on him coming over to you for an unwelcome visit.

If you immediately come out with some snappy verbal assault like, "What the hell are *you* lookin' at!" He will feel compelled to counter with an equally sharp rejoinder, which will then deteriorate into violence.

So, what else do you do? If you were to apply the psychology of Fut Ga, you would confront him casually, but firmly, to diffuse the situation at its start. How? The first thing to do is address his stare immediately, before he's begun to inflate his ego. You might say, "I notice you're staring at me for some reason; do I remind you of someone? Do I have something on my shirt that I can't see? Do I owe you money?" (jokingly).

In this way, you've dealt with him in confidence, something he's unaccustomed to. A man like him is used to dealing with the weak and the bluffers and blowhards (it seems that water actually does seek its own level). Never consider bluffing!

If you point a gun at someone or warn them that you're a black belt, the average man on the block will be properly impressed—but then, he's the one least likely to attack you. The one who will attack you in spite of your claims has heard empty threats before. He will call your bluff, and you'll either talk, fight, or flee.

The best way to utilize your martial art and self-defense training is to take charge of a situation before it becomes a situation. In order to do that, consider the term "self-defense." To successfully defend yourself, you must think of self-defense in its broadest scope. If you're faced with an opponent who hasn't attacked you yet, even though you know an attack is imminent (you know that he's simply waiting for his moment to strike you), shouldn't you attack him first and eliminate him before he becomes a problem?

Self-defense is comprised of two basic actions: defense and offense. What I'm suggesting to you is that very often if your offensive skills are up to par, your defensive skills may be more finely honed as a result.

Offensive skills were first hinted to us by what I like to call our "paternal legacy." Bear with me for a moment while we take a brief trip down memory lane.

There exists in our society a paradox that is really quite amusing. A father will tell his son (as his father will have told him), "Son, always avoid trouble; but if it ever looks like you're going to get into a fight, be sure to get that first punch in. It's important!"

One day in the not-too-distant future from that meaningful conversation, Junior will heed his father's sage advice when the proverbial school bully picks a fight with him. Junior punches said bully firmly in the snout, bully begins to cry, teacher rushes to the scene of the crime, and Junior will be questioned.

You see, his teacher, principal, and yes, even dear ol' dad will inquire ominously with a note of impending doom in their collective voices, "Who threw the first punch?" Junior proudly tells them, and each of the authority figures (whom he's always trusted), will look at this little barbarian and shriek in unison, "You did?" (A pause here for a long look of disgust and bitter disappointment.) "You started the fight? You're going to be punished!" And of course, sadly, Junior will be punished.

It isn't surprising, therefore, that in an encounter where heated words are exchanged and you realize that things are definitely going to become violent, you allow your antagonist to "start the fight," thereby absolving yourself of any wrongdoing when you finally have to defend yourself. This is understandable, but when you do this, your safety margin

will be significantly reduced for every second you stand
before your attacker-to-be.

You see, the longer you stand before him arguing, trying
to decide if he's going to hit you, thinking about what you'll
do when he does, bam! You've just been hit! It happens that
fast. Your mind was occupied with too many things instead
of watching his body for telegrahic movement.

You really only have two proper choices in a potentially
violent situation: fight or leave. Either leave immediately
or fight immediately. Remember, the longer you stay in that
gray area in between, the shorter your safety margin, and
ultimately it will be your indecision that will be your
downfall.

This brings us to what the laws of self-preservation dictate
to us as opposed to what the laws of man prescribe for us.
The laws of man tell us we may only use equal force to
defend ourselves (i.e., if someone shoves you, you may only
shove back). The contention is that if someone pushes you,
you don't have the right to kick him in the groin; doing so
would be construed as excessive force.

In theory, the idea of using equal force sounds good; in
practice, it leaves a lot to be desired. For example, if you're
of average height, weight, and build and are about to be
punched in the jaw by someone of similar size, it will hurt
but you probably wouldn't be severely injured. If, on the
other hand, your attacker were extremely large and powerful, that punch to your jaw might possibly break your neck,
causing paralysis or death. So in this instance you would be
compelled to use excessive force to equal his.

The law of self-preservation dictates that you injure him
by striking a vital area; the law of man would disagree and
you would most likely be jailed (depending upon circumstances). So you see, the extent to which you're willing to
defend yourself will not only depend upon your conscience
and how much injury to inflict, but also the grim prospect
of being incarcerated or sued.

Being a martial artist puts you in an awkward position to
defend yourself in that the populace in general will expect
you to handle any size or number of people with relative

ease. They've seen it done at the movies and on television—
can they expect anything less from you?

This brings us to a dichotomy that exists between what
martial arts in general advocate and what survival in street
practicality dictates.

A question that is frequently raised to me during the course
of anti-rape seminars is whether a 98-pound woman can
actually defend herself from a large and aggressive man.
Maybe, but only if she's willing to go to the extremes that
are necessary. If this 98-pound woman is attacked by a
250-pound young, athletic man who makes known his intent to do her great bodily harm, willfully and with malice
aforethought, she should feel compelled to blind, maim,
cripple, or kill him.

Does this shock you? Are you disappointed I didn't impart
pearls of wisdom and insight as to how this woman might
save herself without hurting her attacker? I don't blame you;
I too wish things could be different from the way things are.
Reality has always been the nemesis of higher ideals!

If the 98-pound woman were a martial artist, she would
be presumed to possess the ability to quickly and efficiently
apply a leverage technique, any number of come-along
techniques, or a combination of lessons designed to
neutralize her attacker with minimal injury to him.

If in fact this woman attempts to facilitate any of the above
techniques to subdue her attacker while at the same time
looking out for her own safety, her margin for error is
increased while her safety margin is significantly decreased!
In short, she cannot afford the luxury of being kind and
considerate to an attacker who is large, powerful, and intent
upon hurting her.

This being the case, we cannot abide by present inclina-
tions toward passivity when it comes to our own self-
defense. Far too often, the concept of passive self-defense
is directly reflected in training.

Ideally, training in the martial arts should cover every
contingency; this being true, shouldn't you spend equal time
training for offensive self-defense? It really wouldn't be all
that difficult; you could begin by defending against your

partner's attack when you see the initial movement of the blow rather than the completed punch or kick.

From there it would be a simple and natural avenue to develop, learn, and practice offensive attacks. The attacks can run the gamut from immobilization (i.e, shin kicks to the side of the knee or thigh), to control techniques incorporating the limbs or hair, to takedowns and holds, and to sudden violent techniques that will neutralize your attacker (finger jab to the eyes, chop to the throat, kick to the groin, neck snaps, etc.).

In the Fut Ga family of san soo, the psychological embodiment of offense technique, you'll draw upon internal power (proper breathing, balance in movement, and sudden execution). And in this more aggressive mode of training, you'll find it to your decided advantage to hone your predator sense. This will seem contradictory to practitioners of traditional forms of martial arts and, of course, it is.

The possibility of a violent attack on your person from a seemingly innocuous encounter with a stranger might not shock or surprise you, especially in light of daily newspaper accounts. But still, just because we can't quite relate to a face in the paper or on television telling us that same tired old ''There-I-was,-minding-my-own-business-when-this-guy-started-stabbing-me'' story, doesn't mean we can't prepare for such an occurrence.

How do you prepare against a knifing, clubbing, or shooting? Apart from wearing a bulletproof vest, helmet, and shield, the best and most expedient way is to attack as the opponent picks up the club or reaches for a knife or gun. Obviously a change of tactics will be called for if the weapons are already in hand; fleeing comes to mind most readily.

Although fleeing is a sound practice when confronted with violence you can escape from, it isn't the answer for everyone. A case in point is a friend of mine who recently informed me that he was now up to his fighting weight; he admitted that he was too fat to run anymore!

If you're in just such a position or have no avenue of escape, you're all the more ahead if you're willing to attack first and last. If the prerogative of passive self-defense is taken from you and you're compelled to initiate the attack and you haven't trained for it, your attack is going to be woefully ill-timed and poorly executed.

To begin practicing offensive self-defense, you will need to apply the fullest extent of your knowledge of the principles of line, distance, angle, and movement. Of these, the most important one to utilize is the distance principle. Correctly applied, the distance principle will give you a decided advantage over a great many opponents without their even realizing it.

As you've learned earlier in the book, when you allow someone to invade your safe distance (arm's length), you can be struck at will; you have too little reaction time to prevent being hit. While this is unfortunate for you, it can also be used to your advantage if you invade your opponent's safe distance and strike first.

To make this more pertinent to you, you can and should incorporate the distance principle as a guideline as to when to strike your opponent. If he's at your arm's reach, you may banter with him as long as you feel comfortable; but if he sets one foot inside your safe distance, then *he* has decided for you that you should hit first.

Establish your safe distance at exactly your arm's reach, no farther and no less. Remember, if you let him initiate a kick from outside your reach, you'll have to deal with the full brunt of the kick rather than the initial movement (Fig. 108a). If he's kept at the correct safe distance, you can stop the kick merely by lifting your knee (Fig. 108b). Maintaining this distance also prevents your opponent from feinting and countering because you will act on his initial movement rather than the completed punch. Remember this if you remember nothing else: to more fully utilize whatever skills you now possess or are in the process of learning, you must assume your opponent is a vastly superior fighter than yourself, but don't give him a chance to prove it! Smother his attack before it can actually be construed as an attack by an observer. In order to best accomplish this, you must launch your own attack at the first signal of his impending

Figure 108a

Figure 108b

attack rather than the completed punch, as many of us were taught to do.

If you allow your opponent to complete his punch so that you can try to intercept or counter him, things might go suddenly dark on you. You will almost certainly get hit if he possesses good speed and power, qualities you were already supposed to assume he has. This being the case, your only viable alternative is to abort his attack when you first feel that he might hit you.

It may seem terribly redundant of me to keep harping about hitting the opponent on his initial movement. I agree; I am being repetitive, but for no other purpose than to emphasize the one thing that is so simple and direct that you can lose the significance of it if you don't apply it. Getting there first is not only important, it's crucial! You must act immediately as you decide on your move; your thought and action must be as one.

To acquire this predatory mode of action, you must learn to stalk with subtlety. You must position yourself with people in front of you in such a way that you'll have a swift entry. Have your partner stand before you as though you two were arguing. Now, without being obvious, watch his feet and, however he's standing, I want you to mirror his nearest foot.

If you stand before someone, most of the time one of your feet will be slightly ahead of the other, and certainly so if you feel threatened; there really aren't that many times when someone will stand before you with his feet together.

Before you continue with this chapter, go and talk to someone and then talk to someone else. As you chat, notice the positioning of the feet. More importantly, notice which foot is nearest you and casually shift your posture so that your forward foot is closest to his forward foot (if his left foot is nearest you, your right foot should be nearest it).

Now, back the the text. I can tell you that in most instances you should move in to him on the side of his forward foot. This is because you can still maintain your safe distance while at the same time have an avenue of entry predicated by the opponent. Your lead foot will be nearest his lead foot, thereby enabling you to have a clean line of entry on that side because of the reduced distance between both of your feet. You'll be behind him, safely away from his punches and kicks.

Now have your partner stand before you with his left foot slightly forward. Of course, you will position your right foot as close to his left as your safety distance will allow. Don't be obvious about looking down at his feet or shifting your position after you've gotten this down; don't even give your partner a clue about what you're doing.

As suddenly as you can, grab the back of his upper arm as you begin to step behind him on his left side. Pull him to you in order to more quickly propel yourself behind him. Once there, you'll be in a position to control him by clutching his hair and pulling his head back, grabbing his throat, or any number of techniques we'll get into later (Fig. 109).

Do this a lot. I want you to practice this particular movement until you gain entry and control of your partner in one fluid movement.

Figure 109   **Figure 110**

Another alternative would be to step directly between his legs with either one of yours, and bind his arms with your hands as you butt him in the face (Fig. 110). The advantage of this entry is that you can enter and pin his arms to his sides with your hands while you head-butt, knee him repeatedly in the solar plexus or groin, pivot him around by using a hair-control technique, or hook his upper arm as with the previous technique. The possibilities for neutralizing your opponent are virtually limitless. Explore on your own what you can do with these entries and then refer to the back of the book for examples of various techniques.

I believe the best argument for using offensive entries and techniques is that when you initiate violence, *you can control the degree of the violence!* It's true; you don't have to destroy your opponent simply because you have control of him. I offer you techniques at the start to show you how to put your man down if need be. But if viciousness can be avoided, you can simply apply pain without injury to make the opponent cease further aggressive behavior.

To do this, go back to the beginning and make your entry alongside your partner. When you do, cup your left hand under his chin (your right hand will pull him in to you if you're stepping in on the right). When you've cupped his chin, pull him in tight and then drop to your right knee. From there, his back will be pressed against your left leg, your left hand will have the back of his head against your left knee, and you can gain further control by gripping his shoulder tightly to immobilize him.

Once you're behind him, you can do any number of takedowns and immobilizations that you can think of (problem solving). In this position, try to reason with your opponent if possible. If he's genuinely amicable at this point, you may release him. If you think he may attack you again as soon as you release him, you can launch a series of blows with your fists, elbows, and knees to the muscles of the arms and legs. In this way, he'll have his arms and legs bound in pain by the charley horse effect you'll have given him. Do this so he won't be able to attack you again.

One of the primary advantages in being able to control your opponent by initiating sudden violence is that you can neutralize your attacker-to-be without bloodshed and a minimum of commotion. While this may not be all that important or desirable in a street situation, it is important if you're in any number of social functions that would be compromised by extreme violence.

Think of it; you already have in your possession the innate and learned ability to overcome opponents you even now feel you can't beat. You can beat them, and I'll tell you why: *you aren't going to give an attacker the chance to beat you!* You'll simply assess what needs to be done, and then do it! Don't argue, don't back up, and don't dwell on what might happen; your thought and action must be simultaneous.

Do you think this is cheating? The simple truth of the matter is, yes, it is cheating in the conventional sense. But there's no correlation between ethics and survival in a suddenly violent situation. Though similar to outward appearances, sport fighting and self-defense are more different than you might think.

Sport fighting has long appealed to our sense of honor and fair play, and that's good. Sports has always impressed upon us the concept of games between relatively equal opponents and discouraged the attitude of gaining unfair advantage over an opponent. These ideals fall under the heading "sports-manship." But as with the rest of our higher principles, values, and ideals, they fall by the wayside whenever the law of self-preservation enters the picture.

By necessity, sport and street fighting must embrace different applicable principles. To better understand what I'm getting at, let's take a look at sport karate. When it's time to fight, the opponents approach each other with sufficient time to plan an attack before they actually close and fight. Each of the combatants has the time to adopt a stance or stalk one another around the ring. Each man is in possession of his circles of influence and center of gravity. When this condition exists, and you allow an opponent the time to "get ready," then you must be ready to endure punishment.

So, if you're going to initiate the fight, you *must* close and occupy your opponent's center of gravity, you *must* move without hesitation, and you *must* leave your opponent in such a way that he won't be able to attack you when you're finished with him.

You will be able to defeat opponents you might not think yourself capable of now, as I've stated earlier, and that will only be because you're using knowledge instead of skills or brawn. But knowledge is a curious thing—think back to a time when you watched someone perform some sleight-of-hand tricks and how impressed you were with them and other magic. Pretty impressive, right? Did you ever learn how some of the stunts were done? The stunts probably weren't so impressive then; once you knew their secrets, you may have felt everyone in the world knew them as well.

Knowledge is power. Your opponent thinks he's able to beat you, but you *know* you can beat him while he's still *thinking* about beating you!

We'll get more involved in the practical application of Fut Ga techniques in Chapter 9, but for now, just know that you don't have to be a magician to defend yourself; you don't even have to be in good shape; all you have to do in order to beat someone who poses a threat to you is to do it! Think about that for a minute; the essence of sudden violence is to do it. Don't make an angry face, don't start bouncing, and don't give any indication you're going to do what you're going to do. Simply establish your safe distance, pick an entry, and then. . .explode!

Chapter 5
___
___

HUNG GA:
THE PHYSICAL
DYNAMICS
OF FIGHTING

In this chapter, you'll begin to put into actual practice and training everything you've learned thus far. The Hung Ga family of kung fu san soo concerns itself with the physically challenging aspects of san soo that will most enable you to become an intelligent fighter.

There are many aspects of the Hung Ga family that I'll be unable to share with you at this time; these aspects concern peripheral areas to fighting, such as forms and dynamic tension. While these areas by and of themselves aren't essential to fighting, they're extremely valuable assets.

For now, you can prepare for a san soo fighting workout by learning to roll and how to fall safely, so that you'll be able to come back *immediately* with a defense or attack after being knocked down.

How to Roll

Knowing how to roll is important in case you are ever knocked to the ground. If you're thrown to the ground, you can conceivably tuck your body to absorb or deflect impact and regain your footing in one continuous motion. The advantages in being able to do this are obvious, but are

Figure 111

especially important so that you aren't injured or have the wind knocked from you, leaving you in a vulnerable position on the ground.

To begin learning a forward roll, step far forward with your right foot. Then lean down and place your right hand, palm down, in front of your right foot, with your left hand placed about twelve inches beyond. Now tuck your head in the crook of your left arm and shove off with your right leg; as you roll forward, tuck your left leg in so that you come up on your left knee and into a standing position, if you have enough momentum (Fig. 111).

The inside of your left arm will protect your head from hitting the ground, and your roll should be felt along your right forearm, to the right shoulder, onto your back, and then onto your left buttock. There shouldn't be just a single point of impact—if that is what you felt, then get your wind back,

Figure 112

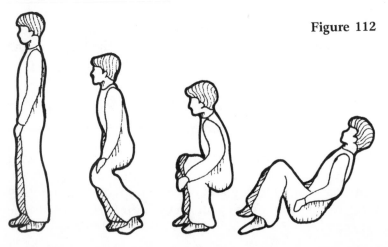

dust off your butt, and do it again.

I know the instructions sound terribly complicated, but believe me, learning to roll properly and safely is well worth the time invested in its learning. Just read the instructions a few times and walk through it step by step until you have it down to one continuous movement.

How to Fall

Once you feel completely at ease with how to roll, it'll be time to learn to fall. Knowing how to fall safely is important (some people would even say it's an art) because if you don't fall correctly you can sprain your wrist, crack your tailbone, or smack your head on the ground.

Any one of these pitfalls is enough to put you on the losing side of a fight if you're knocked down. Once you break your fall, you can roll out of the way and get to your feet, or you can defend yourself while still on the ground.

To begin learning to fall, stand relaxed (on a carpet or lawn initially) and then collapse backward. Once you feel yourself beginning to fall, immediately drop your buttocks to your heels and roll onto your back; when you roll to your upper back, plant your feet and lift your buttocks off the floor as you lift your head and slap the ground with your palms, arms extended (Fig. 112).

By dropping your buttocks to your heels, you put a curve in your back so that you roll onto the ground instead of falling flat and possibly injuring yourself. Your arms splayed to the sides will prevent you from trying to break your fall with your wrists. Also, the extended arms help to better dissipate the shock.

Accuracy

By now you should have a functioning knowledge of observation, distance, timing, technique and balance if you've followed the book and practiced. To begin your initial foray into the realm of Hung Ga technique workout, you'll need a good deal of concentration from both you and your partner.

Of primary concern for your safety when in an actual fighting situation will be concentration on strike accuracy from the beginning of the workout.

Have you ever watched in awe as an enormous man with the physique of Hercules enters a room? We all have, and very often cast a silent prayer that we won't have to tangle with him. But when we look closely at this specimen, we discover that he isn't much different than you and I after all. Despite his size, strength, and girth, he doesn't have muscles sufficient to protect his shins, knees, groin, throat, nose, eyes, spine, etc. So, you see? We really aren't fighting the great mass and bulk, but rather, specific areas of the body. The vital areas and pain centers are the only feasible places you can hit that will neutralize the size and number of opponents.

There are some men who seem to be able to take punches to the face and belly all day long without much effect, and many people are impressed by this. This isn't really quite the feat that it appears when you consider that the average man will throw a looping-type blow that will glance off with little if any real damage. Instead of punching to a *specific* portion of the head (i.e., nose, chin, temple), they tend to close their eyes and say in their mind, "I sure hope this knocks that sucker out!"

You may correctly gather by this that accuracy has as

much importance as speed, power, and awareness in a violent encounter (accuracy will be further explored in Chapter 6). Study the charts in Figures 113 and 114, and strike to these various vulnerable points when your partner attacks you.

Your partner should react as though he had actually been struck, with his head and hands following the pain. It's important for your partner to react in the same way as the man in the street will react to the pain from the delivered blows so that you'll know what control you will or won't have, and so you'll see what portion of his anatomy will be exposed to you next.

For example, if you strike to the groin, the head should lower, thereby making it a simple matter to apply a hair technique that you won't have to reach for, to snap the neck or take him down. Likewise, a punch to the kidneys should tilt his head back in the direction of the blow.

It's important that you work out slowly at first. In this way you can develop accuracy, balance, power, and a degree of fluidity to your strikes and techniques, and your partner can acquaint himself with the strikes you deliver.

This is a two-part proposition; you defend yourself by employing various principles and techniques and seeing what position they will put your partner in, and he'll get an opportunity to react and roll with the strikes as they land (I didn't say it would be a fun opportunity).

Learning to roll with the punches during your workout is important because you'll be able to ride out an attack without feeling the full brunt of the blows. Since it's entirely conceivable you'll be struck in a fight, it would follow that if you can roll with it (as when you're working out with your partner), it will lack sufficient force to hurt you. You and your partner should trade positions as attacker and defender frequently.

Follow-Through Methods

A very crucial aspect of your effectiveness in defending yourself successfully lies in your ability to follow through with your attack after your opponent is on the ground. You

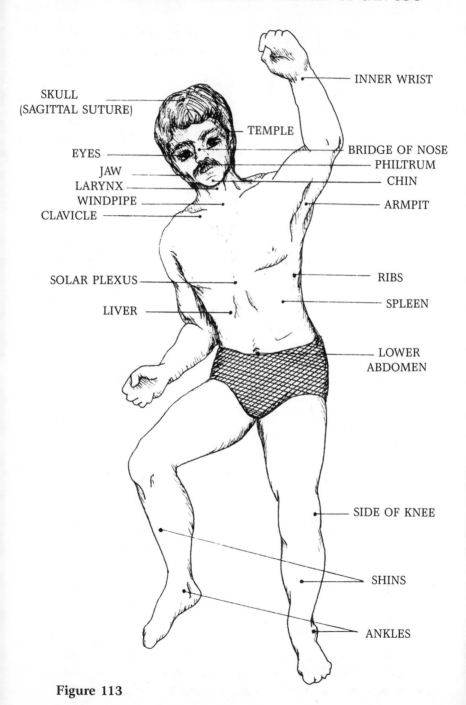

INNER WRIST

SKULL
(SAGITTAL SUTURE)

TEMPLE

EYES
JAW
LARYNX
WINDPIPE
CLAVICLE

BRIDGE OF NOSE
PHILTRUM
CHIN
ARMPIT

SOLAR PLEXUS

LIVER

RIBS

SPLEEN

LOWER
ABDOMEN

SIDE OF KNEE

SHINS

ANKLES

Figure 113

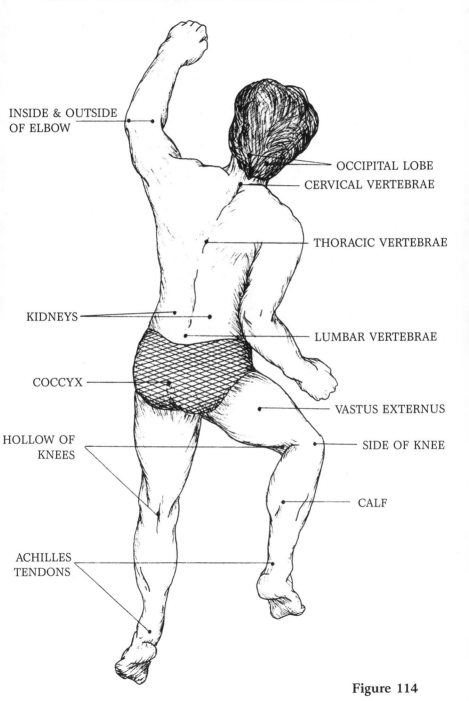

INSIDE & OUTSIDE
OF ELBOW

OCCIPITAL LOBE

CERVICAL VERTEBRAE

THORACIC VERTEBRAE

KIDNEYS

LUMBAR VERTEBRAE

COCCYX

VASTUS EXTERNUS

HOLLOW OF
KNEES

SIDE OF KNEE

CALF

ACHILLES
TENDONS

Figure 114

should bear in mind that because you take your attacker
to the ground once doesn't guarantee you can do it again.

One very good way to keep an opponent from getting back
up and attacking you again is to break one or both of his
legs. To do this, you can stomp on his kneecap (when you
lie down face-up, you can slide your hand under your knee;
this small gap facilitates a good leg break), stomp on his
ankle, or step over both his legs and drop to your knee with
your trailing leg onto one of his legs, pivoting in the opposite
direction and dropping your knee onto his other leg
(Fig. 115).

Figure 115

You can also drop your knee in this fashion onto his chest or midsection to do other damage, and you may also drop onto his neck.

Another follow-through method would be to drop to your knee onto his groin (this will cause his head to rise in pain) and punch into his face at the same time (Fig. 116). This method has an advantage in that when you knock your opponent down, you simply step in again and effect your follow-through. When you drop on him, however, you must be careful of his knee or legs jerking up in reaction to the pain and hitting you.

Figure 116

Any time you kneel down on an opponent, remember to keep your head up; if you lean your head and upper body down when you knee him, your opponent can grab your shirt front and pull you down.

If the attacker has gone to the ground on his belly, you can still follow through in the same way. Another thing you can do if he's down on his belly is to press your knee into his back and pull his head back by the hair or chin to either snap his neck or hold him in place (Fig. 117). You can also slam the head into the ground repeatedly from this position. The possibilities are endless as far as what you can do to keep your man on the ground once you put him there.

I want to leave you with a thought before continuing on

Figure 117

to a different area, and that is to keep vigilant even after you've put your man down hard. Don't leave yourself in a vulnerable position by stepping over him when he still has the faculties to continue punching, kicking, and grappling if you give him the opportunity.

In a san soo technique or combat workout, try to be like a spider going after an insect caught in its web. The spider doesn't just amble over to it and sting it a little, take a rest, and go back again and again. Once the spider makes its move, it doesn't let up until it's completely finished with its victim. So when you've committed yourself to movement on your opponent, don't give him a chance to recover and successfully counter you. Continue punching, kicking, biting, clawing, or doing whatever you have to do until you're finished with him and are confident that he'll be unwilling or unable to attack you again.

Training Tips

Now that you have a few ideas about what to do during a workout, I'm going to walk you through an entire technique and suggest ways to make variations once you have it down. But first of all, study the photographs in Figure 118 and follow these instructions:

1) Your partner delivers you a right punch.
2) Swat his punch aside with your right hand as you kick with your right leg to the side of his knee on the leg nearest you, buckling him.
3) Pull him in to you as your left knee strikes him in the face.
4) When he folds over, strike downward hard enough to the spine with your right elbow to take him down (easy on your partner).
5) When he falls, step over him with your right leg and drop your left knee onto his left kidney.
6) Pivot back and drop your right knee onto his right kidney and spine. Grab his hair, pulling it back to snap the neck or to hold him in place.

Practice this technique over and over until you have a natural feel for it, and then forget it. Don't get bogged down trying to commit a workout technique to memory because there are too many variables involved that will force you to improvise on the spur of the moment. What's important is that you get a feel for the techniques so that you can integrate the block of one technique with the attack or takedown of another and then follow through spontaneously with yet another attack.

Now go back to the technique I just gave you. Instead of swatting his punch aside and kicking, step to the left with your left foot and guide his punch with your left hand; knee him into the solar plexus with your right knee. Follow through the same as before.

You can make further variation by using the swat and kick, then running in place on his solar plexus or groin instead of knee-striking him only once. Finally, follow through by hammering the bottom of your fist to the back of his neck to drop him. Follow that up by stomping him wherever you want. The possibilities go on and on; you're limited only by your conscience, ability, and imagination.

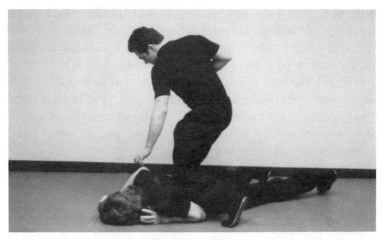

Figure 118

Remember, if you search your memory for a complete lesson or technique when someone throws down on you, you will almost certainly be hit.

When you do make your entry, do not just hit him a few times and spring back into a boxing or karate stance. This is not a sport; this is not a game of tag. It isn't even much fun! Handle each attack from your partner as though your life depended on it.

Now, to begin your workout in earnest, establish your safe distance from your partner. Instruct your partner to throw a punch; when it's delivered you will block, attack, take down, and follow through. For example, your partner delivers a right punch, and you outgrab his punch with your right hand as you step alongside of him to the left with your left foot, close and tight enough to him so that he can't pivot and hit you. You knee him in the solar plexus with your right knee, grab the hair at the back of his head, and drop to your right knee to run his head into the ground (easy on your partner), stomping to the back of his neck.

If you have a preconceived lesson in mind and are anticipating a particular blow, you won't be paying proper attention to his body English. You could be hit while trying to make up your mind which lesson to apply.

So again, it's important that you establish your safe distance and block, attack, take down, and follow through. If your partner closes and invades your safe distance without having been attacked as yet, you should attack, take down, and follow through.

It's desirable to maintain a steady barrage of well-placed and movement-efficient blows to attain an aggressive behavioral mode, particularly if you or your partner are more cerebral than physical. While some may argue that an aggressive attitude compromises one's integrity, I promise you it will be something you can live with.

Be extremely cautious when you apply various techniques on your partner; work out slowly and concentrate on accuracy and well-balanced execution rather than speed and strength. Your lives are quite literally in each other's hands!

At the end of this book will be a list of suggested techniques for you and your partner to practice. Of the ones I'm going to give you, some won't feel natural to you no matter how many times you practice them. In that case, simply eliminate such techniques from your repertoire and use the ones you feel the most comfortable with. You may find, though, that if you make a couple of simple variations of the techniques you feel uncomfortable with, you can make them your own.

Now I'll give you a few suggestions to better round out your workout schedule. First of all, try not to lean into or away from your attacker during the execution of a technique; instead, hold your head up and level. If you need to lower your body during any phase of your workout, let your legs lower you down. This way you'll be better balanced to deal a more decisive blow. Try to keep in mind to always have your head in line with your pelvic girdle (center of gravity).

Next, any time you strike your partner, let your air out as you hit for more power, and concentrate on putting as much body weight as possible behind each blow.

If you're the attacker and your partner strikes you in the solar plexus, let your air out as you're hit to prevent the wind from being knocked out of you. The first instance that you're struck hard in the solar plexus, you'll know immediately that you're not having a good time. To better illustrate my point, have your partner give you a medium-strength punch to your solar plexus as you hold your breath and tighten up. Not worth a damn, was it? After you're able to get your air back, have him punch you again, equally hard, only this time let all your air out at once as you're hit. Wasn't that better?

Some of the movements in these techniques can be carried over into other areas. For instance, you can utilize an open-hand technique into a weapon technique with very little modification. To illustrate my point, let's look at a simple hair takedown.

Have your partner deliver you a right punch; guide his punch past you with your left hand as you step past in and alongside him to the left with your left foot. Then shift your right foot around and behind your partner as you grab the hair at his forehead, and yank down as you drop to your right knee for a takedown (Fig. 119).

Next, have your partner deliver you another right punch. Wrap your belt or similar object around both your hands so that you have a foot length of belt between. Guide the punch past by deflecting the punching arm with the belt and step behind him, then loop it over his head and around his neck. Pull him to you as you drop to your right knee for the takedown (Fig. 120). You can essentially do the same technique with little variation if your attacker has a stick, chain, or knife.

Figure 119

Figure 120

Begin attacking and defending *slowly*, lest you get injured. If you're defending, try to avoid the temptation of doing a technique at top speed; pace yourself to your opponent. If you block or deflect a punch too fast, you could miss his arm or leg entirely and get hit. Go only as fast as your partner, and give his body time to react to each of the blows before going on to the next one.

If you hit the solar plexus or groin and then the nose, give his body just enough time to bend from the blow to the groin or solar plexus before you hit the face. This way, you can put more force into the blow to the head because it will be closer to you.

Incorporate your weapon, ground, holds, kicking, and multiple-attack techniques into your workout so that you can do them instinctively. Then you can overlap one area of training with another—multiple attackers with weapons, ground techniques with weapons, and working out with limitations as though you were handicapped in some way. These areas will afford you ample opportunity to "problem solve" spontaneously with what experience you have gained thus far in the study of san soo and each of its five families.

Work out only as fast as you're safely capable. After a short period of time when you feel completely at ease with the principles of line, distance, angle, and movement, you may begin to work out with your partner dealing full-speed blows. This is where you should peak after each training session, because you're then left with a high-caliber synaptic response to a sudden movement.

At this time, too, you should work on closing the safe distance with each other. By agreement with your partner, and at times during the workout, have him try to invade your safe distance before attacking you. When you see this happening, attack him first!

Strive to maintain positive mental attitude, awareness, decisive techniques, and good humor. Be careful, and good luck!

Chapter 6

$$\blacksquare$$
$$\blacksquare$$

HOI GA: LETHAL ACCURACY

As you start to read this chapter, a very large and powerful man is approaching you. He may be in a car on the way to your house, or at this very moment prying open a window to get inside to murder you; no reason, he just wants to make you bleed—a lot! You have only a few moments to yourself before you have to do anything.

What will you do? You don't have a firearm; a quick look around for an alternative weapon proves fruitless. In desperation you struggle to recall what you learned in your many self-defense classes. No comfort there—you had the lessons but you haven't learned anything tangible enough to give you confidence (too much time spent learning a proper stance, a proper bow, and a proper humble attitude). Better hurry and decide because he's getting closer, and this guy is big!

Too late; he seems to have materialized out of nowhere. He stands there, filling your mind with a brief flash of terror as you think you recognize him. But, no, it was someone else, at the movies brandishing a machete or chainsaw. Not him, but it might as well be.

Your stomach churns and your knees begin to tremble

185

uncontrollably; your heart is pounding and you can hardly breathe. Rallying your last ounce of courage, you assume a stance and scream out a loud "Kiaahh!"

He smiles.

You direct a kick to his groin that glances off his inner thigh. You kick at his kneecap only to hurt your foot when you miss and hit his shin with your toes.

In desperation you punch as hard as you can to his solar plexus, only to hit his upper abdomen instead.

As he leans down to grab you by the throat, you punch his face as hard as you can. His eye begins to swell, but then, so does your hand—it's broken!

If you think that hurt, your big friend is about to give you a new definition of pain. In fact, you're going to suffer more than what he had allowed for you. Why? Because your blows were inaccurate and brought him pain with no injuries. All you've served to do was sharpen his will to hurt you.

Wake up! It was all a bad dream. Since this little drama didn't actually happen, you have time to get prepared in case this nightmare should ever become a reality.

When viewed objectively, the saddest thing about fighting is the fighters themselves. Instead of picking targets that will end the fighting as quickly as possible, one or both opponents will draw back a fist and launch themselves into a blood-and-bruise fest. One or both of them will deliver perfunctory punches and kicks at general areas they've heard were vital areas, and then follow up with a flurry of punches to other generalized areas. Occasionally someone will be hurt, but it'll be due more to accident than design.

As martial artists, most of us pay only lip service to all the ideals, concepts, stratagems, and principles that are supposed to make us the awesome fighting machines almost everyone thinks we are.

Before you begin to shake your head and detach yourself from the rest of us, I'd like to give you a little test of your knowledge of basic anatomy. Ask your partner, spouse, friend, or whomever, to stand before you while you attempt to press your index finger to the points I outline to you.

Locate the following organs: liver, spleen, heart, kidneys, bladder, and lymph nodes (cervical, axillary, inguinal).

Locate the following bones: clavicle, humerus, femur, tibia, fibula, scapula, vertabrae (cervical, thoracic, lumbar), sacrum, and coccyx.

Locate the following veins and arteries: carotid, femoral, brachial, and internal and external jugular.

Finished? These are easy and readily identifiable places of the body that at one time or another are targets that we strike at during the course of an average workout or sparring session. Yet as apparent as these places are to us, more people will miss their exact location than those who'll touch them accurately.

Accuracy, and accuracy training by its own definition, is an exacting process. In the art of kung fu san soo, this important facet of martial training falls within the parameters of the Hoi Ga family.

Hoi Ga is the study and application of pressure points, pass and crippling points, vital areas, and the ways and means of striking them to bring about pain, injury, or death. This is a facinating area of martial art exploration, because when you know where to hit and how to hit there, *you will become a living weapon!*

Does that sound too dramatic to you? Then consider this: if you were to encounter a man wielding a .44 magnum pistol, you would naturally feel apprehensive and possibly a little fearful. The man with the pistol will see this reaction in you and might possibly think to himself, "Yeah, I'm bad everyone's afraid of me because I'm sooo dangerous!" Well, as a matter of fact, he is dangerous, only because he's *holding* a deadly weapon!

The difference between you and him is that *you* are the weapon. After having trained in san soo, you'll know how to use your body to gain more power than you knew you had; you'll also know precisely where to hit to bring to bear more destructive force than your opponent could ever possibly imagine! You see, unlike the man with the gun and a false feeling of power, your weapon is your knowledge and a very tangible feeling of confidence that reveals its presence like a beacon to those accustomed to dwelling in the dark side of life. If you don't believe this now, you soon will (you're still learning).

The one attitude adjustment you most need to make in order to feel totally free to be the weapon you truly are, is this: *dare to be ruthless!* Does this surprise and disappoint you? It shouldn't really. I, too, subscribe to the universal martial tenet of respect and consideration for our fellow man, but when my fellow man attempts to attack me and hurt me for whatever reason, he ceases to become someone worthy of kindness and respect. He simply becomes a collection of target areas held together by meat, bone, blood, and gristle!

When you get right down to it, few of us can really afford the luxury of prolonged combat against significantly larger opponents, multiple attackers, or attackers with weapons. We have to make each and every blow count for all it's worth, lest we be mortally struck and become someone's fond memory, or crippled and someone's burden.

When you're defending against someone who's truly large and powerful, each and every blow he delivers can have the potential of permanent damage. You therefore can't allow him the time or opportunity to deliver any strikes at all. If just one of his punches should land at or near the temporal lobe, you might not wake up for a long, long time or you might wake up dead (now there's a cosmic thought).

If he hits your torso or abdominal cavity as hard as he can, the potential for internal bleeding and broken ribs is too great to dismiss just because you might be a black belt and he doesn't realize how awesome you are. If any of his blows land, he never will know how awesome you are because you'll never be able to prove it—you'll be crippled!

Now that I've gotten you depressed and angry at me because I haven't written quite what you want to read, I'll suggest ways you can train to better protect yourself against people you don't want to meet.

First of all, get some general and specific information about human anatomy. Second, put that information to work. For instance, locate a certain organ, bone, artery, vertebrae, or joint, and incorporate entries and strikes that will get in the quickest with the very most power you can put into it.

Consider punches that utilize the most body torque, kicks you can put your weight into, and other body surfaces you can best hit with to a certain area. Then attack the vital area you're after so you can hit it consistently from whatever angle your opponent attacks you from. Stay with that one target and deliver repeated blows with different striking tools. Consider this a training exercise.

A vital point is an area of the body where shock to the nerves or internal organs can best be facilitated. There are three types of vital points in the application of the Hoi Ga family of san soo; they are nerve centers, pressure points, and pass points.

A nerve center is a small area with a concentration or cluster of semiexposed nerve endings that are highly susceptible to a variety of strikes to produce pain, particularly pinching, clawing, finger jabbing, and gouging.

Not all concentrations of nerves are considered vital points, and striking a vital point does not necessarily produce the same effect in each case. For instance, if you pinch one man under his upper arm or inner thigh with a certain amount of pressure, you'd have enough control over him with this alone to do with him what you want; with another man, you'd have to pinch a lot harder and/or take advantage of the opening he'll allow you when he reacts to the pain.

A pressure point is a medical term that adequately describes the vulnerable areas, particularly vascular junctures. In a martial context, a pressure point can be an organ such as the eyes, kidneys, or spleen, or muscle groups and bone surfaces that are immediately responsive to a strike, such as the nose, spine, tendons, or biceps. Very often, vital and pressure points can be one and the same (eyes, groin, larynx, etc.).

Pass points are entirely neural in content and involve permanent crippling injuries that are inevitably fatal. The pass point is a topic that doesn't lend itself well to a book format without there being personal instruction far more

extensive than I'm able or willing to do at this time. The
application and responsibility of this facet in Hoi Ga training
falls into a gray area in the art of san soo that is quite simply
too esoteric for me to even begin to share with you without
my knowing who you are. For what you're learning with
this book, you don't need to learn about pass points. The
principles, application, and knowledge of vital and pressure
points are more than enough to meet your needs.

Take the time to briefly study the body charts in Figures
121 and 122 to get an initial feel for where you're headed
when you begin your workout applying accuracy skills.

You'll need to have your partner stand by, wearing an old
but snug T-shirt and a pair of swimming goggles. Now begin
to outline your own technique that will involve a variety
of specific target areas.

For example, you can either execute a Fut Ga technique
by initiating an attack, or block and make an entry after your
partner attacks. You can strike with a left finger jab to the
eyes (touching the goggles, of course), followed by a right
punch to the spleen, then a left punch to the liver; you can
then grab him by the hair and force his head down and right-
chop the back of the neck (specifically the occipital lobe at
the base of the skull and top of the cervical vertebrae).

While all this may sound like a bit too much, enjoy; you're
in a learning process right now, and you're literally exploring
your way over the human body in a way that is truly unique.

When you set up a series of targets and a systematic way
to hit them to make your opponent bend, drop, fold to the
left, topple backward, etc., you will want to implement a
variety of strikes (Tsoi Ga). You'll also want a variety of ways
to find and incorporate a leverage to a particular area (Li Ga)
with a variety of entries for sudden attack (Fut Ga), all the
while utilizing the workout format as a vehicle to bring these
facets into being (Hung Ga). Then, of course, you'll want
to hit with deadly accuracy (Hoi Ga). And there you have
it, the five families of san soo at your fingertips.

Recall that little drama at the beginning of this chapter
and rewrite it to account for what you would do now. When
you do this, think to what ends you can go to generate

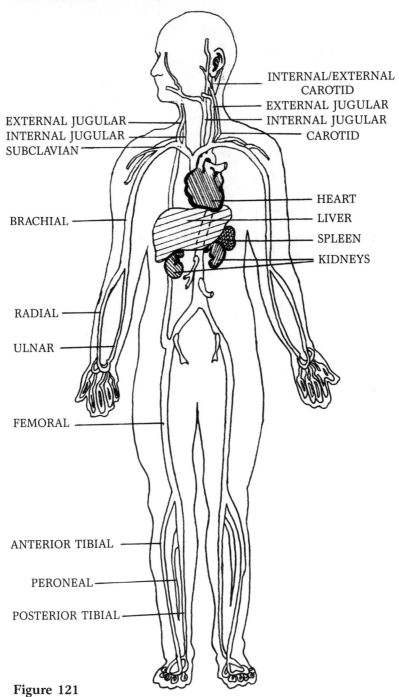

INTERNAL/EXTERNAL
CAROTID
EXTERNAL JUGULAR
INTERNAL JUGULAR
CAROTID

EXTERNAL JUGULAR
INTERNAL JUGULAR
SUBCLAVIAN

HEART
LIVER
SPLEEN
KIDNEYS

BRACHIAL

RADIAL

ULNAR

FEMORAL

ANTERIOR TIBIAL

PERONEAL

POSTERIOR TIBIAL

Figure 121

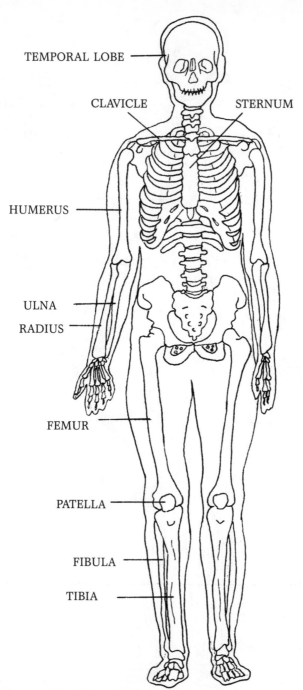

TEMPORAL LOBE

CLAVICLE

STERNUM

HUMERUS

ULNA

RADIUS

FEMUR

PATELLA

FIBULA

TIBIA

Figure 122

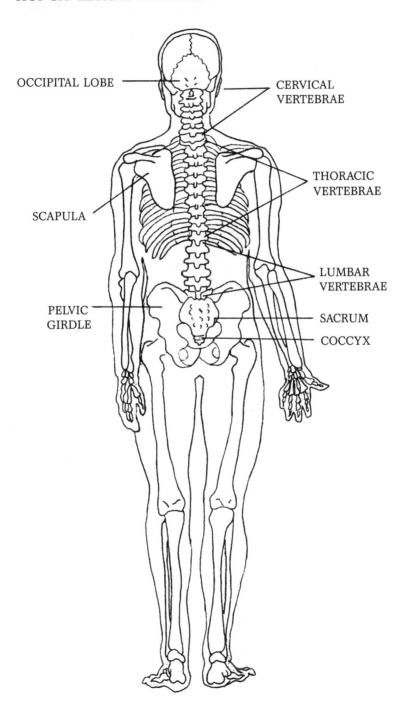

OCCIPITAL LOBE

CERVICAL
VERTEBRAE

THORACIC
VERTEBRAE

SCAPULA

LUMBAR
VERTEBRAE

PELVIC
GIRDLE

SACRUM

COCCYX

sudden extreme pain for your opponent.

Uh oh, you won't have to recount that scenario after all; that big ugly fellow I mentioned is standing behind you right now and has every intention of turning you into a puddle! It seems the ball is in your court now—*what will you do?*

Chapter 7

WEAPONRY FIGHTING

Before we get involved actually training in the principles of defense against weapons, I feel this is the time for a brief discourse about just what a weapon is and when it is truly a weapon. In this way you'll have a better understanding of what actually poses a threat to you.

If you place a gun, knife, club, chain, machete, and straight razor on a table, you would simply have a small group of inanimate objects. These objects do not become weapons simply by being picked up. Each can become a serious weapon only when someone of reasonable skill and intelligence handles them in a manner for which they were designed, and uses them in conjunction with a reasonable amount of judgment gained through experience. This done, whichever object this person picks up becomes a weapon.

For example, I'm not a marksman; if I were handed a high-power rifle with a powerful scope and were asked to hit a target the size of an elephant or the proverbial broad side of a barn at 300 yards, chances are extremely remote that I would hit it. However, if someone who is skilled in this area were asked to do the same, shooting at an even smaller target, he would almost certainly hit it. The rifle in his hands could be considered a deadly weapon. That same rifle in my hands at that range would simply be a loud noisemaker. This being the case, it would naturally follow that a weapon can only be as effective as its user.

Moreover, a knife in the hands of an experienced knife fighter is truly a deadly weapon. To someone else, it's simply a sharp and pointed object that could hurt someone. It's only an inanimate object until you learn to make it a weapon.

What makes all this worth relating to you is that if you have a functioning knowledge of self-defense principles and can direct whatever object you have in your hand to an opponent's vital area, having a better sense of body movement and awareness than he, you can be better armed with a ballpoint pen or even just your index finger than an unknowledgeable opponent with a butcher knife.

One of the first principles to know when dealing with someone with an object/weapon is to realize what the *actual* threat to you is—in other words, don't worry about the gun, worry about the bullet! It's in this light that you must know that the person holding the object should be considered the weapon. The knife is just an extension of his body (a frightening extension).

Knife Defenses

We'll begin your training in weapon defense with defenses against a knife and then progress to other weapons. To begin, get a stick or similar object that can serve as a knife, give it to your partner, and square off. When you defend from his attacks, you'll be using an equal amount of body and hand movement.

Have your partner take some swipes and stabs at you with the artificial knife while you try to fend him off. Do this right now for about ten minutes.

When I witness one of these encounters, it's like a scene from a bad movie played over and over. If yours was a typical encounter, your partner would be stabbing and swiping at you, feinting and lunging, while you crouched down with your arms forward and apart as though hugging an invisible tree.

You probably tried to slap the knife out of his hand or to kick at it. But whatever you did, and if your partner was sincere in his attacks, you will have been repeatedly sliced about the wrists, arms, legs, and feet. And all the while you tried to dodge and deflect him, you were continually leaping back and away from his lunging stabs. If this is true of you, we'll have to change your way of thinking before we delve into any of the knife defense techniques.

Consider for a moment when you were the aggressor with the knife against your partner. You watched him and noticed that his movements were contingent and dependent on you. You will also have noted that with his defensive posture—crouched and sort of running in place with his arms forward and apart to parry your attack—he will have offered you several targets to cut until you could press in for the final attack and kill.

Foremost with everyone, regardless of the art, style, and years of training, the law of self-preservation takes precedence over any and all lessons or techniques. Your initial reaction would and should be to run and get away from the knife; that's spontaneous and seems to be the correct thing to do *at the time.* However, if your attacker is just barely out of arm's reach, you won't be able to flee quickly enough to prevent getting stabbed in the back if your attacker pursues you. Go back again with your partner and try to escape, and you'll see that this is true.

Correct distancing is of paramount importance when defending against a knife attack. Essentially, distancing will be the same as if he were unarmed (arm's length). You'll need to be in a relaxed posture with your arms at your sides as though you have no intention of defending yourself. If the opponent makes several feints and jabs at you outside your safe distance, let him. When he's ready to get down to business, he'll bring himself to you. At this point, he'll come within the effective range for you to employ the san soo principles of line, distance, angle, and movement of attack.

198 SUDDEN VIOLENCE: THE ART OF SAN SOO

Now, have your partner take the imitation knife and stab at your midsection in a lunging motion. As he does this, pivot your body sideways, facing the inside of his stabbing arm. As you pivot, swing the back of your right wrist (if your opponent has the knife in his right hand) to the inside of the wrist that is holding the knife (Fig. 123). Strike sufficiently hard to dislodge the knife.

Figure 123

If you attempt this technique by relying on hand motion alone, you may be able to disarm him, and by pivoting sideways into him, you won't present yourself as a target should your hand technique fail. When you pivot your body at the same time as you strike his inner wrist, you'll gain sufficient body power behind your blow to smash the veins and nerves in the wrist to cause the fingers to release the knife.

Another technique to use against a stab or prodding of a knife would be to bow your midsection back when you strike to maintain a safe distance as you effect your hand technique. In this case, strike directly down on top of his wrist with your fist or to the top of his forearm with the bone portion of the bottom of your wrist (Fig. 124).

If the opponent is making a horizontal slashing motion at you, the technique illustrated previously (Fig. 123) is a good one to employ, provided you follow up with a counterattack of your own immediately after you disarm or neutralize the weapon hand. With any of these defenses, you should not give the attacker an opportunity to attack again.

Figure 124

If the attacker should stab downward at you, pivot sideways and slap-grip the top of his wrist or forearm and continue it on its path; if the technique goes as it should, he'll stab himself.

Once you and your partner feel comfortable with these techniques, dip one end of a small stick in a bit of ketchup or other coloring agent, and really try to stab-touch each other with the stick. I know it sounds foolish, but it'll put you in a competitive frame of mind to see if you have the necessary movements down.

As you practice, make the variations in technique you feel most natural with while establishing and maintaining your safe distance, acting upon his initial movement in to you.

Do not at any time during the course of your weapon training begin to joke and play around with your partner; you'll both suffer for it at some later time if you do.

There are more defense techniques against blades, and they all have merit. I have illustrated just a few so that you may practice them well enough and be flexible enough to make your own variations while staying within the framework of your movement principles to do what needs to be done. It's far better that you're able to do a few methods well, with room for spontaneous innovation and problem solving, than to vaguely know several techniques.

Before leaving the topic of knife defense, I'd like to stress the importance of assuming a predatory attitude at the first hint of danger. Take the responsibility to be suddenly violent! Don't wait so long to defend yourself that you're in a position to have to parry repeated slashes and stabs. Once you get an idea that an opponent even has a knife, utilize a Fut Ga technique to abort his option to attack.

Stick Defenses

The next area of weaponry we'll delve into will be defense from sticks. Whether it be a nightstick, tire iron, or any other type of bludgeon, remember to fight the man and not the object.

When you're accosted by a man wielding a club, your initial response might be to run or back away. As mentioned previously, this is a natural response when confronted with any weapon.

The first lesson to learn and internalize about defending against someone with a stick is not to retreat. While you may elude getting hit once (twice if you're exceptional), you'll eventually be hit if the opponent is really trying to hit you. To better understand why, have your partner hold a length of hose or other object that won't hurt so badly if you get hit by it. Then, as with the knife defense drill, have him swing the object down onto your head or shoulder as you try to back up or run away from it. You will find that if your partner is really trying to hit you, he will.

Change roles now and try to hit him before he can get away. Change yet again. This time, as he lifts his stick to bring it down on you (or as he begins his swing), move in on him, and the stick will swing down behind you (Fig. 125). & 125b).

The last few inches of the stick is what will inflict the most injury to you; so even if a blow glanced off you while you're moving in, it won't be as hard a hit as if you had dealt with the length of it. The force of the center of the stick would

Figure 125

be painful for sure, but not as injurious as the end of the stick!

Next, have your partner swing at you horizontally. As he starts his swing, step in to him so that you're face-to-face, controlling his striking arm to continue on its path in the direction he was swinging. When this is done properly, he'll pivot his body around yours as he continues his swing; his body should drop at the end of his spin when he loses his balance after having fallen over your leg (Fig. 126). Execute this movement quickly and decisively when you first detect his swinging movement.

Before we continue into the next method, I'd like you to consider an easier alternative to these techniques. That alternative is to simply watch and act. What this means is that when the majority of people swing a club, they'll draw it back to hit you. At this point, the general consensus among most martial art styles is to defend against a delivered blow.

This is a wrong attitude when defending against someone with a weapon! If you encounter someone who draws back to hit you, blast him *as* he draws back. Alertness and decisiveness play a key role in doing this, and should you fail to hit him in time, you may follow through with any of the techniques in this section.

This next technique involves increasing the opponent's momentum when he swings at you. Have your partner direct a blow downward to the top of your head. As he swings down on you, step in to him and continue his striking arm in a downward direction. If done correctly, he will hit himself (Fig. 127). This is an ironic as well as an effective technique, in that as hard as the opponent tries to hit you, he will hit himself instead.

If an opponent attacks you with a staff, pole, cue stick, or any other long-stemmed object, you can utilize essentially the same techniques as in stick defenses. Get a broom handle or staff of some kind and we'll begin.

First of all, take turns attacking each other in the same manner as with a stick and defend in the same way. Get the feel of working and making variations to suit the added length of the weapon.

Figure 126

Figure 127

Having done that, have your partner swing at you horizontally and crouch in and below the object as you move in
on him. Then have your partner stab the pole at you, aiming
for your midsection. As the staff approaches you, pivot

sideways as in the knife defenses and guide the staff past (Fig. 128). Then move in and attack him.

Experiment with different attacks with the staff, and incorporate the principles of line, distance, angle, and movement in addition to the variations of defenses. If I showed you fifty lessons on how to deal with a staff, stick, knife, chain, etc., that's exactly what they would be—lessons. If you're forced to think for yourself and problem-solve, then you can arrive at your immediate solutions spontaneously! Believe it or not, you already have your answers.

Figure 128

Chain and Belt Defenses

Chains are a popular item with street gangs and thugs; after all, who else would just happen to have one on them? At any rate, a belt is pretty common on a man's waist and can and often is used in the same fashion as a chain. You could encounter either one or something similar one day, so it would pay to know what to do should the occasion arise.

As with a stick, most people will draw back their arm to hit you before they actually deliver the blow. They don't know any better, and you should take advantage of them. With a limp object such as a chain, most people will feel the need to put it into motion so that they can work with it; this motion is normally a backward swipe to straighten the chain out and build up momentum for the blow. When this happens, abort the movement by attacking your opponent (Fig. 129)!

Figure 129

You may also incorporate the defense techniques of the stick and staff to avoid getting hit with the chain. The last few inches of a chain, as with a stick, are what will hurt you most.

When you defend against a chain, you must remember to keep the swung chain in motion rather than interrupting the movement. If interrupted, the chain will wrap around what interferes with its path of movement. So, if you must defend from a chain, attack as the opponent draws back to hit you. Also, if you duck under the chain, you can punch up into the groin in the same movement (Fig. 130).

In addition to this technique, you may also step in deep and pivot your body in the direction he's swinging to keep the motion flowing.

Figure 130

If it happens that you disarm an opponent with a chain and have to defend against other attackers or if you're confronted by someone with a club and you have the time to remove your belt, you can use both weapons in the same way. Stretch the belt (or chain) between your hands about shoulder distance apart to ward off or deflect the other weapon. If you hold the chain loose between your hands and then snap your hands apart, the flexed chain will repel the attack and leave the opponent exposed (Fig. 131).

If you're going to swing your belt or chain at an attacker, simply step forward and bring it up into the blow from wherever it lay.

There are plastic decorative chains on the market that would be safe to realistically practice with. With a plastic chain or suitable substitute, you and your partner can swing at each other hard and fast enough to take each other seriously.

Knife Attacks

Since we've gone over various ways to defend against these weapons, it seems only logical that you have a

Figure 131

functioning knowledge of how to use them yourself. Once you disarm an opponent, you may need to know how to use the weapon against other opponents.

The first one we'll work with will be a knife. If you're going to use a knife against someone right now, you will hurt them; after all, knives stab and they cut. However, if you hold the knife in the fashion illustrated in Figure 132, you'll be able to punch with the butt of the knife as well as stab and slash with the blade.

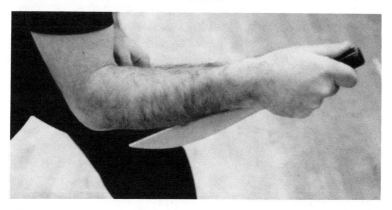

Figure 132

Rather than holding the knife blade-forward and poking it at your opponent, giving him an opportunity to disarm you, I suggest you hold the knife as I've illustrated and use your other hand to feint or ward off his attack (Fig. 133).

Figure 133

A good knife fighter's weapon should be felt and not seen! In this way your weapon is outside your opponent's immediate reach and you'll have your knife in an advantageous position to slash upward and across and to hook and stab. Do not attempt to clash knives as you may have seen in the movies, but rather slice at points on his body where you will inflict the most damage most quickly. End the fight! Instead of cutting across the chest or raking the face, cut where there are major arteries, tendons, and ligaments, like the wrists, insides of the elbows, inner thighs, sides of the neck, throat, etc.

While the prospect of cutting someone in these places is truly a gruesome thought, I feel it's even more gruesome to think of your attacker cutting *you* in these places. If you feel your life is in danger, you will need to produce the highest degree of pain, in the shortest amount of time, with the least amount of effort. Locate and study a chart of the vascular system, and one of organ placement.

If you aren't sure if your opponent really means to maim or kill you, then it isn't necessary or legal to go to the extreme of taking a life. Bear in mind, though, that very few people who attack you with a knife will itemize the extent of the damage they're going to inflict. If you'd rather not stab or cut him, you may still stab with the butt of the knife to the vital areas and follow up with other hand and kicking techniques.

Staff Attacks

If you have a penchant for playing pool and have need to use your cue stick as a weapon, or if you're using a broom or rake at the time you're attacked, you can utilize that object as a staff. To use a staff or long stick, you can utilize one of two methods best suited for your particular instance.

You can hold the staff at the very end to prod, thrust, and whip at an opponent. While this method has an advantage in that it can keep an opponent at a distance and effectively strike him, it also has a disadvantage in that if an opponent gets past the end of your staff, your position will be jeopar-

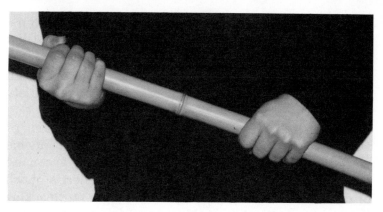

Figure 134

dized. You must then either drop the staff and fight or recover as best you can.

You can also hold the staff near the center as depicted in Figure 134. While you may hold the staff with both palms facing the same direction, the method illustrated is more versatile. With the staff held in this position, you can jab, hook, parry, and slash with relative ease. You can utilize this grip on any long-handled object that you may have in hand or nearest you.

I suggest both you and your partner get a wooden dowel of five- or six-foot length as used to hang clothes on in closets. Wrap the staff in tape so that it won't splinter and get in your eye, and then practice line and movement principles with it.

Don't strike as hard as you can at first when you practice jabbing, parrying, and slashing; you can accidently get hurt too easily. What's important is that you get a natural feel for the staff in your hands and the body movements that will give you best power, mobility, and ease of entry. Be creative in your practice.

If you're using the staff as a cue stick, hold it vertically in front of you with one hand in a relaxed manner. Grasp the upper end of the staff about ten inches from the top and have your partner throw a punch at you. When he punches, you can deflect the blow with the top of the staff and follow through with a punch to the face (his, not yours!) with the staff still in your hand. You can even lift up on the staff and strike him in the groin with the bottom as he approaches to hit you. After you've struck, you can follow through with the staff held in the center to incorporate a wider variety of strikes.

Whether you use a short staff, nightstick, baton, or whatever falls within that realm, you'll have a formidable weapon and many ways to use it. For openers, you can use it to crack an attacker across the wrist to deflect a punch or disarm a knife, or you can initiate a fight by smacking the stick across the knees, shins, or other areas to limit his mobility and create pain.

You can use the stick to effect a simple takedown by grabbing both hands to the bottom of the stick, hooking behind the head, and dropping quickly down to one knee (Fig. 135).

You can hold the stick with a hand at each end to deflect punches and kicks (Fig. 136). With the stick held in this fashion, you can hit effectively and painfully to the face,

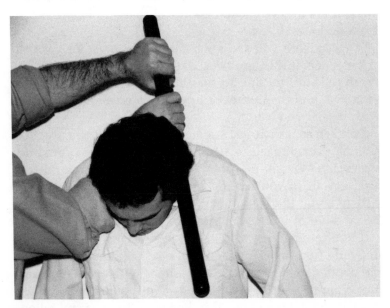

Figure 135

Figure 136

throat, diaphragm, and external joints. You can hook it over
an attacker's head and pull him to the ground, and you can
use it in this way to uppercut under the chin or slam down
on the knee.

You can use a tightly rolled newspaper in much the
same way as a stick; only with a newspaper, you're much
better put off jabbing with it. You can use it to deflect a
punch or kick, and you can use it to jab the face, throat, or

Figure 137

groin. Rolled magazines can be used in this fashion as well (Fig. 137).

Other Weapons

Additional items that can serve as weapons are keys, books, and purses. These items are usually near at hand and can be readily employed; other less handy items that can be used run the gamut from paper clips to ashtrays. You are limited only by your imagination, the item's accessibility, and how hard or where you hit with it.

With keys, you can stab to the soft places like the eyes, throat, and other pressure points shown earlier in the book. You can always scratch or claw at strategic places with keys; it's usually a good idea to have them in your hand as you approach your house or car, anyway.

When entering or leaving a library or going to a class at school or college, you will often have in your possession at any given time, a weapon that is much more formidable and versatile than you might realize—a book.

You can hold a hardback book in such a way as to utilize its surfaces to your advantage (Fig. 138). You can jab edge

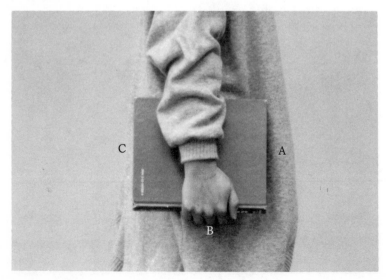

Figure 138

A into the face and throat or up into the groin, or use it as you outgrab a punch and jab the edge of the book up under the elbow to break the arm. You can use surface C to chop down on the collarbone, the back or side of the neck, or other areas where the opportunity presents itself. You can still punch with the book in your hand (surface B) where and when a target presents itself on your opponent, and you can

Figure 139

also use the flat surface of the book to smash into the face (Fig. 139). Experiment and see for yourself how many different ways you can use a book other than for reading.

You can also use a purse or handbag to your advantage. You can swing it up into the groin (Fig. 140) or alongside the

Figure 140

head to stun, following through with another technique.

You can also use the carrying strap in your favor by swinging the bag around behind an attacker's head and grabbing it to pull his head down and knee to the face (Fig. 141).

Figure 141

Experiment and see what else you can do with it.

The usage of weapons is an interesting if not fascinating study in and of itself; you can and should consider further training in this area. My aim insofar as this book is concerned is to acquaint you with a basic knowledge of movement skills that you can readily adapt spontaneously, without getting embroiled in strategies that won't have time to work in a sudden violence situation. If I were to address the text of this book specifically to the weaponry techniques of san soo, you wouldn't be able to apply them nearly as well without having learned the fundamentals of the art beforehand.

As I've stated earlier, the brevity of actual techniques and the variation of applications allow you to better modify the techniques and make them conform to your particular abilities and temperament.

I'll end this chapter on weapons fighting by giving some unneeded advice—do not get involved with a weapon carrying person in the first place, if you can possibly avoid it. But, if you must, don't be so intimidated by the object that you become immobilized by it. If you have trained as you should, *you'll be better prepared for a violent encounter than your attacker!*

Chapter 8

███████
███████

SAN SOO
AND CHILDREN

Children the world over, in all walks of life, share a common bond; they are and always will be easy victims. They will be attacked by other children, teens, and adults. The severity of the attacks will range from pushing and slapping to molestation, a savage beating, and even murder.

No parent can state for certain that their child will never be attacked or abducted. While it's true that a large number of children do grow up without having been beaten or molested, it's also true that attacks on children are on the increase and nobody knows whether their child will be a statistic. This is a sad commentary on our society, but that's the way it is.

If you have children and are thinking of relating the things you've learned from this book with them, I suggest you be very selective of what you teach them. Children as a whole lack the discretion of adults. If you were to teach your child the entire contents of this book, chances are that the first time another kid stuck his tongue out at him or her, your child might poke him in the eye or kick him in the groin. If that prospect doesn't bother you, then consider this: you are financially responsible for your child's actions. The following story will bear this out.

I used to work as a conductor for a railroad in Southern California; one of the men I worked with was also learning san soo. His ten-year-old son was being harassed by the proverbial school bully, who would tear the boy's shirt off whenever he had the chance.

The man had only recently begun training and thought it would be a good idea for his son to take lessons as well. The boy was enrolled in a children's class, in which different aspects of self-defense were emphasized. The man thought to supplement the boy's training with what he had learned in the adult class. This proved to be an unfortunate and costly decision.

It wasn't long before the boy was again confronted by the bully. When the bully grabbed the boy's shirt front to tear it off, the boy applied a wrist and arm leverage to its fullest extent. The leverage locked the arm out, twisting and shoving its length into the torso. The result was a fractured wrist and a splintering of the forearm that left permanant impairment.

The injured boy's parents sued the man for a very large sum of money that will seemingly take an eternity to pay. All this because the son was taught a technique he should never have learned. He hadn't the slightest idea of the medical implications of the technique. Because of the son's anger and frustration at the bully, it's understandable that he would apply the lesson hard enough to assure his being left alone in the future.

I'm sure that had the boy known what the consequences would be as a result of the technique he applied, he would either have chosen a different technique (that he would have learned in a children's class) or simply lost his shirt. At the expense of an injured boy (even though he was apparently a rotten kid), we can all learn from this.

It's ironic that despite the frequency of beatings, abductions, and molestations of children in this country, they could have a very good chance of escape by utilizing adult techniques of self-defense—the very thing we have to worry about them using on other children.

This is a very delicate and controversial area to delve into; while the child has the potential of defending himself, the child stands the chance of bringing more injury to himself if the attempt fails. The degree of potential varies from one child to the next, and so, too, the ability to utilize the principles and techniques. In this light, I'll illustrate a few techniques and possibilities. Extreme discretion should be exercised by the parent whether or not to disclose these techniques to their children; always advise them of the consequences, medical and otherwise.

There is a multitude of variables involved in children's self-defense. Far be it for me to dictate any hard-and-fast rules for action or nonaction in any one case. One of the variables to consider is the proximity to other people at the time of the assault. That is to say, if other people are near or within hearing, the child would have a better chance of escape if he failed to effect the technique properly or at all.

If the child were to be accosted in a secluded area, it's questionable if he or she should resist at all. While the child may hurt the attacker enough to escape, the attacker may overtake the child and add a beating to whatever else he had planned to do.

Bearing this in mind, it would be a good move on the part of a parent to take the time to inform a child of the existence and intents of a molester. In this way, a child can have an awareness of the dangers of talking to and following strangers. I believe young children have a greater capacity for understanding than we give them credit for.

If you decide to teach these techniques to your child, be absolutely certain they understand the dangers involved in using them, on other children as well as adults.

The first technique a child can accomplish without too much difficulty is an ear cuff. If an attacker picks the child up around the waist with the child facing him, the child can cup his hands and smash the ears simultaneously (Fig. 142). If this is done hard enough, it can rupture the attacker's eardrums. It can also cause him to lose equilibrium, thus affording the child an opportunity to escape, and it can also

Figure 142   **Figure 143**

cause hemorrhaging by concussion.

If you intend to teach this technique to your child, hold a basketball in your palm and have the child practice palm slapping to the sides of the ball in the manner described above. Impress on the child to hit hard!

Another good strike your child can do to effect a release from the same position would be to palm-strike upward into the nose (Fig. 143). This could break the cartilage of the nose and cause a great deal of bleeding, as well as flooding the eyes with tears and swelling them shut. As you can well imagine, this will cause a great deal of pain. The child can repeat this strike as hard and as often as necessary.

From this same hold, the child can sharply ram his forehead forward to smash the attacker's face, repeating the blow as fast and continuous as need be. If this same hold is applied with the child's back to him, the child can strike with the back of the head to the face (Fig. 144).

If the attacker grabs the child by the wrist or arm, you can teach the releases covered earlier in the book. Additionally,

Figure 144

the child can bite the attacker's wrist or hand hard enough
to effect a release. Have the child practice this technique on
you with just enough effort to escape. If the child tries as
hard as possible, you could be hurt; convey this to the child
before you start.

Pushing, tackling, and headlocks are among the most
common attacks a child can expect from other children. You
can refer to the chapter on Li Ga to show the child defenses
from various attacks along those lines. As for pushing,
instruct the child in the principles of distance and telegraphic
movement. Then have the child face you and prepare for
a push. Do this exercise with your partner first if you wish,
because pushing can be a prelude to a fight even in the adult
world.

If you're being shoved with one hand, move your shoulder
back as you're being pushed. If it was a hard push, the
opponent should lose balance when he meets no resistance,
thus leaving himself exposed and vulnerable.

When being shoved with two hands, you can slap the

Figure 145

nearest arm aside so that it crosses over the other one and
guides past you (Fig. 145). As with the previous technique,
this can take the opponent off balance if he shoves hard
enough and you direct him aside. Too, he should be exposed
and vulnerable to your attack.

When an attacker tackles you, you'll both end up on the
ground. To prevent this from happening, you should take
action at the first hint of a tackle. As soon as you see the
attacker drop his head and/or crouch, be prepared to deal
with a tackle. There are those who will telegraph a lot, and
there are those who will give you little warning, if any, at
all. As with every technique, be alert.

Practice and have your child practice so that neither of you
have to search your memory for what to do; you won't have
time to think about it.

If you recognize in time that you're going to be tackled,
kick hard to the head or chest to take some of the steam
out of the attack (this is more appropriate for adults than
children), or you can sidestep and direct him past you; then
take him to the ground with you in control. You can do this

by placing one of your forearms on the back of his neck and the other one under the chin, and then dropping to your knee or belly (Fig. 146). You can then hold him there or turn him over and press your attack. Dropping to both knees after grabbing his head before his arms wrap around you is also a quick method of takedown.

If you make only a half-hearted attempt at a strike or technique, you won't bring sufficient pain to bear to effect control or escape. It will only serve to enrage the opponent to hurt you more than he may have intended. So again, if you do a technique at all on an actual attacker, do it hard!

I mention this in this chapter so that you'll relate it to your child. It's especially important for the child to use as much force as that little body can muster for the reasons mentioned above.

If your child expresses an interest in learning more, it would be to your mutual benefit to teach him. If you do enroll your child in a class, be supportive. Many parents enroll their

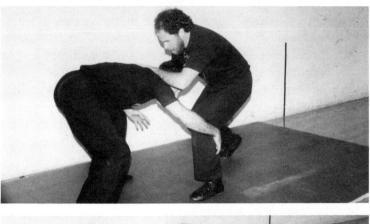

Figure 146

children in martial art schools and have expectations for exceeding the child's or instructor's capabilities. While it's true that the child can learn to have self-confidence, it takes time, as does learning balance, coordination, and self-defense skills. Children are notorious for their short attention span and not finishing something they've started. Be patient.

Very often, a parent will enroll a child in a class under the pretext of the child's betterment, when in fact the school serves as nothing more than a regular baby-sitter (rather than serving as strictly a place of instruction). If your motives are truly in the child's best interest, take an interest in the child's class. Give your child your support and show him or her that you're interested in their progress. Give them a chance to show you what they've learned; you'll be rewarded.

Unfortunately, there are those parents who will build their child's confidence one minute, and destroy it the next. A child's ego is a fragile thing, and he or she is of no threat to you! Many a parent will crush a child's budding self-confidence by threatening to spank them "if they try any of that karate stuff" on them. Ridicule, no matter how innocent it may seem to you, can be a devastating blow to a shy child's confidence and self-image.

Try not to imply to your child that he or she is falling behind in your expectations; they have their own expectations to live up to. It's unrealistic to demand that they be the best in the class, but you can encourage them to attain their "personal best."

If you train them at home yourself after having read this book and possibly having trained in a school, you know what they are capable of and what they can and can't be trusted to learn. Just remember above all else to be patient with them. You'll both be glad you were.

Chapter 9

SUMMARY
OF PRINCIPLES

Below is a summary of kung fu san soo principles of fighting that you've read and dealt with earlier, with a few others that might be of help to you, too.

1) Decide at the start of an encounter whether you're going to fight or leave, and then do it!

2) Keep an opponent at your "safe distance" (arm's length) so that he'll telegraph his intent and give you sufficient time to act.

3) Stand relaxed and try to remain calm. Don't commit your arms and legs by assuming a stance of any kind. You can be hit while settling into a stance.

4) Be alert to an opponent's body English. If he settles his weight and makes a fist or any other clue that he's going to hit you, then drop him!

5) Be aware of who is within your reach, and position yourself accordingly.

6) If time allows, think like a predator—*stalk* to gain or invade an opponent's "safe distance," *mirror* his posture, *image* him for movement, and then *attack!*

7) Strike vital areas only (how hard depends on the situation).

8) Strike without telegraphing, and hit with your body weight behind each blow. Hit hard!

9) Once you begin an attack, continue punching, kicking, clawing, and hitting until *you* are through with *him*.

10) Don't be concerned about making an attacker angry if you kick him in the groin. If you do it hard enough, he'll be in too much pain to be concerned with you.

11) Don't worry about winning or losing. Simply defend yourself to the best of your ability.

12) Punch or kick *through* an opponent, not just to him.

13) Don't be reluctant to pick up an object to use as a weapon if the situation warrants it.

14) If you're a woman, don't give in to modesty. If you're wearing a tight skirt and you want to kick, then pull the skirt up and kick the hell out of him.

15) When forced into a violent encounter, create the highest degree of pain in the shortest amount of time with the least amount of effort.

16) Don't be intimidated by a man's size or appearance: they conform to the same laws of physics and pain as anyone else. Simply view each opponent as a solid, mobile area of potential targets, and deal with each of them accordingly.

17) Always be aware of your surroundings and the limitations involved (i.e., stairways, phone booths, crowds, etc.).

18) A smiling face can lull you into a vulnerable state, while the person behind it can attack you as suddenly and savagely as anyone else. Be alert!

19) Utilize an opponent's clothing to your advantage, as in throwing him to the ground.

20) If you're picked up and carried, don't panic and struggle if you can't think of what to do; he'll set you down soon enough. You can then effect an escape.

21) When utilizing a hair technique, remember to slide your fingers through the hair along the scalp and then clutch, instead of simply grabbing the hair in your fist.

22) When dealing with an attacker with a weapon, realize that it's the attacker you're fighting and not the weapon.

23) When confronted with a chain or belt, try to keep the motion going whichever way he strikes, or duck it entirely.

24) When attacked with a club or chain, the last four inches will do the most damage. So if you move in on him and are struck lower than that, it will be with less energy.

25) When attacked by more than one person, don't waste any time on each attacker; maim or strike a vital blow so that you won't have to do it again.

26) Be careful when working out with your partner so you don't injure each other. Work only as fast as you are safely capable of; your lives are literally in each other's hands.

Chapter 10

___

SUGGESTED WORKOUT TECHNIQUES

The following is a list of suggested techniques for your workouts. Make whatever variations in technique that you feel most comfortable with. After you've become accustomed to the various facets and many different variations you can incorporate into your workout, you can try practicing on different terrain, wearing loose clothes, barefoot, or wearing heeled shoes.

As I stated in previous chapters, by no means should you attempt to memorize all of the following techniques. Remember the ones that suit you best and forget the rest. Practice them as they are given, make your own variations, and use them when time and opportunity seem right.

I would like to draw your attention to the usage of the horse stance positions. As I've repeated throughout the text that there is no need for stances, the full- and half-horse positions should *not* be construed as a preparatory or fighting stance! I use them in the description of the following techniques to better illustrate the direction your body should be heading, as well as giving you an idea of how to move in on your man in a balanced position. In this way you can either pivot in another direction when you've hit, or hit as you pivot for more body power. You can modify this position as you're doing a technique.

The photographs for the full- and half-horse positions are in Chapter 2, Figure 47, for reference of position. As long as you can shift easily into a reasonable facsimile of the horse position in a well-balanced posture, that should be all that is necessary to do what is required without establishing the rigid posture depicted.

Half of the following techniques will be for defense from an attack, and the other half will be for offensive attacks (Fut Ga).

For the sake of brevity in the description of the techniques, I'll abbreviate often-used descriptive words and terms. Listed below are the abbreviations and their meanings.

ABBREVIATIONS

(L) Left	(LUW) Left Upward Windmill
(R) Right	(RUW) Right Upward Windmill
(LHH) Left Half-Horse	(LDW) Left Downward Windmill
(RHH) Right Half-Horse	(RDW) Right Downward Windmill

Defensive Techniques

1) Opponent grabs your shoulder with his (L) hand:
   A) Step in with your (R) foot and (R) hammer his arm away;
   B) (R) backhand to the throat;
   C) (L) punch to the ribs;
   D) (R) snap kick to the groin.

2) Opponent delivers a right punch:
   A) Step past him to the left with your (L) foot into a (LHH) as you outblock with your (R) hand;
   B) pivot to a (RHH) as you (L) roundhouse punch into his kidney;
   C) pivot to a (LHH) as you (R) roundhouse punch to the liver;
   D) (R) roundhouse kick to the face.

3) Opponent delivers a right punch:
   A) Step in with your (R) foot between his legs as (L) hand deflects into his upper (R) arm and you (R) hammer down to his nose;
   B) pivot to a (LHH) and shift in deeper as you (R) hammer down into the groin;
   C) pivot into him and (L) knee into the face to knock him down;
   D) drop to your (R) knee and punch into the groin, as (L) hand protects against his leg coming up.

4) Opponent delivers a right punch:
   A) Step in with the (R) foot as the (L) hand outgrabs the punch and your (R) hand chops to the right side of the neck;
   B) wrap your (R) arm around his neck to break or choke;
   C) reach down between his legs and grab the inside of his (L) leg;
   D) pull up on his leg as you push down on his (R) shoulder, stepping around to the left with your (L) foot to throw him down.

5) Opponent delivers a right punch:
   A) (L) hand outblocks as you step into him with your (R) foot;
   B) step over his (R) leg with your (R) leg as you (R) hammer to his collarbone to take him down;
   C) (R) kick the groin.

6) Opponent delivers a right punch:
   A) (L) hand outgrabs to the left as you (R) snap kick to the groin;
   B) step between his legs with your (R) leg as you clap both hands to his ears;
   C) double-knee him (L) then (R) into his groin;
   D) (R) hammer to the back of the neck to take him down.

7) Opponent delivers a left punch:
   A) (RDW) to the right as you step in with the (L) foot;
   B) (L) chop to the throat as you step in to him;
   C) (L) snap kick to the groin;

D) (R) knee to the face.

8) Opponent delivers a right punch:
   A) (L) hand outgrabs to the left as you step in with the (R) foot and (R) backhand to the nose to stagger him back;
   B) (L) snap kick to the groin or solar plexus to fold him;
   C) set your (L) foot down to the left as you (R) claw, roundhouse fashion, to knock him down; stomp his knee.

9) Opponent delivers a right punch:
   A) (LUW) as you step in with the (L) foot, the (L) chop to the (R) side of the neck;
   B) (L) backhand to the bridge of the nose;
   C) (R) hammer to the (R) collarbone;
   D) (L) punch to the (R) ribs, then (R) snap kick to the groin.

10) Opponent delivers a right punch:
   A) Step in and to the left of him as you crouch low under his punch to (R) roundhouse punch into his groin;
   B) kick with the bottom of your (R) foot into his upper thigh, either leg, to take him down;
   C) step in and stomp on his (L) ankle to break it.

11) Opponent delivers a left kick:
   A) Pivot sideways into him as you (R) vertical forearm strike his leg to your left—this should spin him so that his back is to you;
   B) slap down hard to his shoulders with both hands to takedown;
   C) drop your (R) knee onto his chest to pin him as you (R) hammer strike to the groin.

12) Opponent delivers a left punch:
   A) Step past and to the right of him with your (R) leg as you guide his punch past you with your (R) hand;
   B) pivot to a (LHH) as you (L) backhand the back of the neck;
   C) (R) punch to the temple;
   D) step over him and drop your (L) knee into his kidney.

13) Opponent delivers a left punch:
   A) (R) outgrab to the right as you step in to him with the (L) foot and clutch his throat with your (L) hand;
   B) (R) knee him to the groin and then drop to your (R) knee to bring him to the ground;
   C) (R) kick to the face.

14) Opponent delivers a right punch to your abdomen:
   A) (R) hammer strike down on his forearm as you step in to him with the (R) leg;
   B) (R) hand then chops across to the throat;
   C) grab the back of his head with your (L) hand and pull him in to you as you (L) knee him in the solar plexus;
   D) (R) hammer blow to the back of the neck.

15) Opponent delivers a right punch:
   A) (L) outgrab to the left as you step in to him with your (R) leg to (R) uppercut with your elbow to his chin or jaw;
   B) strike downward with your (R) elbow to the sternum;
   C) strike down with your (R) forearm on his (L) collar and grab the hair at the back of the head;
   D) step around and to your left with your (L) foot as you pull down on his head to take him down, then kick to the ribs.

16) Opponent delivers a left punch:
   A) (L) outgrab to the left as you step alongside him to the right with your (R) leg, pivot to a (LHH) and (R) hammer down with your forearm to the back of his (L) elbow;
   B) (R) backhand to the nose as you pivot to a (RHH);
   C) (L) kick to the groin;
   D) (R) punch to the temple.

17) Opponent rushes in to tackle:
   A) As opponent gets to you, strike to the back of his neck with your (L) hand, drop your (R) leg back and (R) elbow strike to the spine between his shoulder blades;
   B) reach under to cup his chin with your (R) hand and

pull up on it to turn him over;
C) (L) palm strike to the nose.

18) Opponent delivers a right punch:
   A) (L) hand outgrabs to the left as you step in with the (R) leg and (R) hammer to the collarbone;
   B) wrap your (R) hand around to grab the hair at his (L) ear or grab the ear itself;
   C) step back with your (R) leg and pivot to a (RHH) as you pull back with his hair to turn the body and bring him down; (L) punch to the face.

19) Opponent delivers a left punch:
   A) (L) hand outgrabs to the right as you (L) snap kick to the groin;
   B) (L) hand claws down to the face, then your (R) hand reaches along the back of his neck to cup the chin on the (R) side of the face;
   C) step back with your (R) leg as you pull up on the chin and pull him to you, shifting to a (RHH) to expose his neck;
   D) (L) punch down to the left side of his neck.

20) Opponent delivers a right punch:
   A) Step to the left of him with the (L) foot as you guide the punch past with the (L) hand;
   B) pivot to a (RHH) as you (L) elbow to the kidney;
   C) pivot to a (LHH) as you (R) elbow to lower ribs;
   D) (L) forearm hammer to both kidneys as you shift to (RHH);
   E) shift to the left again as you draw your (R) leg up and launch it back between his legs to take him down as you (R) chop to the throat.

Offense Techniques

(Fut Ga)

Before you go on to the techniques to initiate a fight, I would caution you to do these techniques only if you're absolutely certain there's no way to avoid a conflict. Name calling, taunting, and insults do not constitute a legitimate excuse to beat up someone. Considering the nature of these techniques, you'd better know without a doubt that your opponent intends to hurt you and that you have no other alternative but to initiate violence.

When you practice these techniques, invade your opponent's safe distance, thereby cutting down on his reaction time, and apply your technique with a high degree of suddenness. Go through the motions with your partner slowly until you're familiar with the technique, then execute it as quickly as you can.

1) Step in to your opponent with your left foot:
    A) At the same time, claw/gouge to the face with your (R) hand;
    B) (R) knee into the groin;
    C) step back with your (R) foot, hitting with a (R) forearm to the back of the neck.

2) Step to the left of the opponent with your (L) foot:
    A) (L) backhand claw to the face;
    B) (R) forearm to the side of the neck as you place your (R) foot outside of his (R) foot to throw him to the ground;
    C) kick to the face.

3) Step in to the opponent with the left foot:
    A) (R) palm strike to the chin as your (R) knee to the groin;
    B) (L) punch to the temple;
    C) grab his head with both hands and (R) knee into the face.

4) Step to the left of the opponent with your (L) foot:
    A) grab the opponent's right arm at the shoulder and pull him in to you;
    B) (R) knee into the solar plexus;
    C) (R) backhand to the back of the neck.

5) Step deeply between his legs with your (R) foot:

    A) Pin his arms to his sides before he can lift them, and head butt into the face;

    B) (R) knee into the groin;

    C) (R) elbow strike to the temple.

6) Step to the left of him with your (L) foot:

    A) Grab opponent's (R) wrist with your (L) hand, then grab behind the elbow with your (R) hand and pull him in to you;

    B) (R) knee into the solar plexus;

    C) (R) chop to the back of the neck with your wrist.

7) Right roundhouse kick to his (L) ribs:

    A) Without putting your foot down, kick to the groin or lower abdomen;

    B) (R) backhand to the neck;

    C) bring your (L) leg around and behind his (L) leg, and (L) elbow strike to the throat.

8) Step on opponent's left foot with your (R) foot:

    A) (L) elbow strike to the heart;

    B) (R) kick to the back of his (L) knee to buckle him;

    C) (L) kick to the groin followed by a (R) kick to the face.

9) With (L) foot forward, slide your (L) arm between his (R) arm and side as you (R) knee to his pelvis:

    A) Bring your (L) hand up to capture his (R) arm and grab his hair at the top of his head with your (R) hand;

    B) step across in front of him with your (L) foot and throw him over your (L) hip down to the ground;

    C) step over him with your (L) foot and stomp his head or neck with your (R) foot.

10) Step between his legs with your (L) foot as you strike to the sides of his neck in a chopping manner:

    A) Bring your (R) leg around and in front from behind his (L) leg and force him down by the shoulders as you bite hard on his nose or cheek, keeping hold of his head;

    B) (L) knee into the sternum.

11) (R) snap kick to the groin and grab the hair on top of

his head with your (R) hand:

    A) Without putting your (R) foot down, pull his head down to (R) knee him in the face;

    B) shove your (R) leg between his legs and against his (L) leg to spread them as you force his head down between them;

    C) step over his back with your (L) leg and drop all your weight onto his back as you hammer to the spine and kidneys.

12) (R) roundhouse kick with your shin to his (L) leg above the knee:

    A) Grab and pull his (L) arm to you with your (R) hand as you set your (R) foot down behind him;

    B) as your (R) foot sets to the ground, grab his hair at the forehead with your (R) hand and pull him back over your (R) leg;

    C) pull his head back farther to expose the throat so you can bite or chop it.

13) Step into him with your (R) leg:

    A) Cup his chin with your (L) hand as your grab the hair at the back of his head with your (R) hand;

    B) drop back to your (R) knee as you twist his head to the right to turn him over and take him down;

    C) you can then either twist the head sharply to the left to snap the neck, or you can force his head forward and down so you can step over his (L) shoulder with your (L) leg and drop your body weight on him to break his back.

14) Step in to him with your (L) leg:

    A) Slide your fingers through his hair at the sides of his head and use your wrists to lever his head backward and down;

    B) step over his (L) leg with your (R) leg to force him down at your feet;

    C) head-butt into his upturned face.

15) (R) punch into the solar plexus as you step between his legs with your (R) foot:

A) Grab the hair at the top of the head and pull him down;

B) run in place with your knees hitting him in the face;

C) (R) forearm blow to the base of the skull.

16) Kick (L) and (R) to each of his knees:
A) Grab the sides of his head so you can head-butt him in the face with the top of your forehead;
B) step your (R) leg between his and behind his (L) leg;
C) (R) elbow strike to the (L) side of the neck.

17) Step between his legs with your (R) foot:
A) Grab him around the waist to trap his arms to his sides;
B) batter him (R) and (L) with head butts to the sides of his face;
C) knee-strike him in the groin repeatedly;
D) grab the hair at the top of his head to expose the back of his neck and strike with your (R) forearm.

18) Step between his legs with your (R) leg:
A) Thrust your (R) index and middle fingers, together, into either eye;
B) kick with your (L) shin to the outside of his (R) knee.

19) Step into him with your (R) leg as you cup his chin and grab the back of his head with the other hand:
A) Step back with your (R) foot and snap the head sharply to break the neck.

20) Step to the right of him with your (R) foot as you pull his upper arm to you with your (R) hand to get past and behind:
A) Cup your (L) hand under his chin and snap the head back as you (R) elbow strike the back of the neck or head;
B) (L) punch to the temple.

These are merely suggested techniques for you to practice to acquire movement skills. Some of these techniques are designed to injure, while others are designed to maim or kill. It's for you to decide where you'll draw the line in how far you're willing to hurt someone.